The Importance of Transcending Spiritual Clichés and
Living Their Deeper Wisdom.

Copyright © 2019 by Rampant Feline Media

All You Need is Love?

All rights reserved. No part of this publication may be reproduced, distributed, or transmitted in any form or by any means, including photocopying, recording, or other electronic or mechanical methods, without the prior written permission of the publisher, except in the case of brief quotations embodied in critical reviews and certain other noncommercial uses permitted by copyright law. For permission requests, write to the publisher, addressed "Attention: Permissions Coordinator," at the address below.

Rampant Feline Media

www.rampantfelinemedia.com

ISBN: 13: 978-0-9998354-5-6

CONTENTS

INTRODUCTION

I Want to Feel, Goddammit

By Chris Grosso

"Without access to true chaos, we'll never have true peace.
Unless everything can get worse, it won't get any better." — Chuck Palahniuk, *Choke*

Give me a quote like the one above from Palahniuk any day over the sappy rhetoric I read from the majority of "spiritual" people, teachers, or whoever-the-hell else, that plasters the internet and social media these days and I'll be one happy camper. I want raw. I want real. I want visceral. I want to *feel*, goddammit, and not just the lofty, ecstatic-states spirituality many (if not most) spiritual teachers and books promise these days, but also the gut-wrenching heartbreak and despair that's unavoidable in life. Do I prefer ecstasy to pain, joy to sadness? Of course, I do. I'm not a masochist. But I am an experienced realist and recognize that to know pain is to know pleasure, to know heartbreak is to know love. We can't know one in its fullest depths without experiencing the other in its fullest depths as well.

I'm currently reading Jeff Brown's latest book, *Grounded Spirituality*, which is one of the most refreshing "spiritual" books that's crossed my path in quite some time. To be honest, prior to Jeff's book, it's been roughly eight months since I've read anything remotely "spiritual." I'm glad *Grounded Spirituality* found me when it did because it prepped me for *All You Need Is Love*. Both share an underlying premise that spirituality is not only about "good vibes," meditation, yoga, transcending the ego, states of bliss, plus a lot of horseshit that's been far too popular for far too long (Quantum Love, Quantum Child-Rearing, Quantum Orgasms, Quantum Abundance, you get the picture). Instead, what you read in both of these books is

1

that while yes, you will experience bliss and joy and all sorts of other lovely experiences along "the path," which is great. But if you're being real in your practice (whatever that looks like for you), you're also going to experience feelings of shit, depression, sadness, anxiety, emptiness. If you're really lucky, you may even feel like you're going crazy, because that's just part of the deal of being real about this stuff. It's also a big part of the reason I love the saying, "It's okay not to be okay." It's okay to have a dedicated practice and your life still be a hot mess. However, with time, patience, and working vulnerably with some kind of practice (again, whatever that looks like for you), the mess *should* begin sorting itself out over time, sometimes quickly, sometimes slowly. But if you stick with it, it will happen.

I say this confidently, as I come from a place where I've nearly died several times due to drug and alcohol addiction as well as suicide attempts. I've been in jail cells, emergency rooms, detoxes, rehabs, psychiatric hospitals and wards. I've pissed, vomited, and shit blood (on multiple occasions) and that's just the tip of the iceberg. But during my times of sobriety, I stumbled onto what some might call a "spiritual" path. Seeds were planted, techniques were learned, words by many of the great illumined teachers were taken to heart. Still, even with all of this motivation and inspiration, I would often return to old habits and behaviors, each time ending in worse conditions and consequences.

The reason I share this part of my life with you, is to exemplify what a complete shit-show my life was, and still, at times, can be (just not in the same way or to the same severity). I still sometimes struggle with depression and anxiety. I still occasionally think a drink or a line of coke would be a good idea. And I still have occasional thoughts of self-harm, or suicidal ideations, though not ones I'd act on in any way. That's just the nature of what I live with. Even after twenty some-odd years of "spiritual" practice, therapists, and more, this ugliness still rears its ugly head periodically.

Welcome to being human.

The beauty, though, is that it's significantly less these days due to my practice and the integral ways in which I incorporate well-being into my life. That and the fact that my "spiritual materialism" phase (a phrase coined by Buddhist scholar Chögyam Trungpa Rinpoche) ran its course rather quickly. I realized early on in my journey that all I was doing was changing my ego's wardrobe. I was "spiritualizing" it and had a brand-new identity to show off. I wore the malas and om shirts. I learned the lingo and the popular mantras. I burned incense and read the most popular spiritual books everyone was talking about. Let me be clear, there's nothing wrong with any of the aforementioned, including the ego itself. It's not the enemy most spiritual teachers make it out to be *if* it's understood for what it is and there's a healthy relationship with it.

At times, I still wear "the gear" and burn incense etcetera, but not to impress anyone or try to make myself seem more spiritual, coming across as something I'm not. On the few occasions I do it now, it's because I feel a sincere connection, or, dare I say, heart-calling to do so. It's like spiritual icon Ram Dass said, "The spiritual journey is individual, highly personal. It can't be organized or regulated. It isn't true that everyone should follow one path. Listen to your own truth."

One of the many reasons I respect and am excited about *All You Need Is Love* is that it shines a light on so many of the popular spiritual myths (or to be more blunt, straight bullshit) that are taught and spread around in many spiritual circles—from the "5 Steps to blah blah blah articles," to positive thinking, enlightenment, ego, miracles and more, this book shies away from none of it. What's great though, is that it's not that *All You Need Is Love* simply trashes these ideas and topics, but rather, takes a respectful, yet no-bullshit approach to exploring them, in many cases, showing that they're not always cracked up to what they're supposed to be.

Now, I don't want to come across as some judgmental, holier than thou, pretentious prick. I went through, explored, and lived basically everything this book covers. I think, to a certain extent, that everyone who sets out on a spiritual journey does. The whole "spiritual materialism" thing is a rite of passage in a way. However, if real progress is to be made, there needs to come a time and place where we become willing to get raw, vulnerable, and take an honest and unflinching deeper look within ourselves. What underlying stressors or minor discomforts have we become complacent with on a daily basis to the point that they're now normal for us, thus we ignore them? What traumas or difficult life experiences are we scared to face? What's really going on and who are we really?

Sure, we can meditate and transcend pain (physical, mental, emotional, and spiritual), which will help for a while. But all too often meditation, too, becomes just another means of aversion and escape, very much like excessive use of drugs, alcohol, food, sex, and shopping. Yep, spirituality and its practices can be an unhealthy addiction!

But (and this is a very big but), if we're willing to do the uncomfortable work of looking at all this shit that's stored up inside, much of which is probably unconscious at this point, then we're truly on our healing journey. And I highly recommend doing this work with some kind of trained professional. Whether it's a therapist, trusted spiritual teacher, group therapy, a combination of these things, or something else professionally. This is not easy work and has a chance of doing more harm than good if not processed in a professional manner (which several chapters in this book point out).

Which brings man back to Ram Dass's earlier quote about "listening to our own truth." When we do the work honestly and rigorously, we become intimate with what our personal truth is. As far as my own direct truth and experience goes, Spirit (or whatever you'd like to call it) imbues literally everything. It's as much in the Buddha or Ganesh statue as it is the dumpster out back of your job or apartment. Bringing this introduction to a close, as I look around my apartment, I have a crooked grin on my face thinking about how my fiancé and I often joke that anyone walking in here, whether they've read any of my books or not, would most likely *not* believe it's an apartment inhabited by a "spiritual" person.

There are collectible horror movie prints on the walls and horror figures basically everywhere. There's a Baphomet statue along with two stuffed, plush Baphomet's. The bookcases provide homes for books on serial killers, psychopaths, and occultism. You'll see skateboards and plenty of musical equipment obviously geared towards heavier music if you happen to be a musician and know what you're looking at. Skulls and bats are a staple of our décor. Essentially, it looks like Halloween in here.

My iTunes consists predominately of punk and hardcore music, underground and old school hip hop, gangster rap, metal from practically every genre, and yes, some kirtan, jazz, folk, and old country (Johnny Cash, Hank Williams etc.). The DVD/Blu-Ray collections are a "cult classic" fan's dream, shelving films from brilliantly twisted minds such as David Lynch, Quentin Tarantino, Dario Argento, John Carpenter, Gus Van Sant, Larry Clark, and George A. Romero.

Yet there are also pictures and statues of Kali, Ganesh, Hanuman, Christ, Buddha, Maharajji (Ram Dass's guru) and more. The bookcases not only include psychopathic material, but also classic texts from the world's great wisdom traditions, including The Bhagavad

Gita, The Dhammapada, The Vedas, The Upanishad's, The Gnostic Gospels of Christ, as well as works from more contemporary-ish spiritual teachers such as Ramana Maharshi, Ram Dass, Pema Chodron, Jed McKenna, Ikkyu Sojun, Tara Brach, Ken Wilber, Pema Chodron, Nagarjuna, Thich Nhat Hanh and more.

For me, this is my truth—my "spiritual" truth—and I couldn't be more comfortable in it regardless of what anyone else thinks. My hope is that as you read the pages of *All You Need Is Love* it helps you become more comfortable in your own truth too, whether you choose to call it "spiritual" or not. I mean, at the end of the day, who really gives a fuck anyways? It's all just life doing its thing regardless of what we humans think about it. So just be cool and don't be a spiritual asshole, okay? High fives all around.

Yours in Spirited Mischief and Love,

Chris Grosso, author of *Indie Spiritualist, Everything Mind,* and *Dead Set On Living*

June, 2019

Chapter 1

One of the biggest clichés to rock the New Thought movement, this quote is wrought with shame and guilt. Trouble is, it's based in truth, because yes, ultimately you are responsible for how you feel. However this saying (and others like it), seems to lay all the blame for feeling miserable about how someone else treats you solely in your lap without considering the other person. It takes two to tango. Yes, you can choose not to feel a certain way. But who does it serve to feel guilty about feeling bad and upset on top of everything else when you've just been screwed over?

GOING BEYOND SPIRITUAL GLIBNESS

It's meme's like this that inspired me to want to create this book. Look, I've seen this quote and others like it floating around social media for years. I'm sure there is more to it than basically blaming people for their feelings and how they react to situations. I'm sure there is a much deeper, longer, and more nuanced explanation of what this quote actually means. Probably an entire chapter or two, or maybe even a book of wisdom about the idea of letting go of the hurt caused by others, understanding our own feelings, where they come from and how to process them—triggers, beliefs, our past story and how they all impact our present experience—all of that and more.

Sayings like this are a byproduct of social media and, by and large, I think, the "self-help" world (okay any arena in this world—we've become a sound-bite society). We all want to want to be quotable purveyors of short, easy-to-read, eye-catching phrases that sound really really spiritual that can be quickly passed around, building up our social and spiritual credibility. Readers benefit too. By writing a deep, meaningful "I am really listening" comment, they, too, can be deemed really really spiritual. And then we all get to go about living our lives (apparently with the permission of an ever-wise and formidable guru or New Thought leader), playing the asshole, saying and doing whatever we want because how other people feel is not our problem.

I doubt whoever wrote this meme meant to give permission for an asshole free-for-all. And sure, I could read this as meaning I am responsible for my own feelings and it doesn't matter what other people do. That I should be a master and not care, or—and here's a big buzz word—I should "transcend" the slings and arrows of life. Okay, that's fair. And yet I haven't met a person (or a self-styled guru, for that matter) who has actually achieved this sense of total disconnection from the emotional vulnerability of their humanity 100 percent of the time—or even 20 percent of the time.

Plus, I have met many a "newbie—the "I took the weekend seminar and now I'm spiritual" woman or man—who reads these kinds of quotes and doesn't yet understand the nuances. They don't "get it," and thus they feel empowered to follow up abusive behavior with a casual "I'm sorry you feel that way" response. They really believe that any amount of asinine, thoughtless, emotionally-damaging behavior is okay because, "Well, your feelings are your feelings and I'm not responsible for them. I read it in a book, or heard it at that weekend seminar. I get to do and say whatever I want! And if your feelings are hurt, that's your problem!"

I believe the concept of taking personal responsibility for how we affect others has become a lost art, especially in the "New Age" community. And with quotes like this being vomited across the internet, it's no surprise.

Of course, if I'm being honest, I admit that I, too, have condescendingly uttered the "I'm sorry you feel that way" line. But that was before I remembered something my dad taught me. And that is: "You are 100 percent responsible for your actions and your words because they have consequences." Which means, if I am an asshole to you, then guess what? Your feelings are very much, in fact, my responsibility.

Missing the subtleties

This quote also includes the idea that how we feel is often based on our past experiences, our beliefs about the world, our trauma's. It directly implies that we listen with filters based on the past and learned beliefs—

9

that it's possible we might hear something one way without understanding it was never intended that way.

These are the kinds of nuances that are often lost when we pull quotes like this out of context and plaster them all over our social media pages. And sadly that's where most people these days stop reading. Everyone is looking for the 3 Easy Steps to Everything (including myself), and using quotes like this is part of that dynamic, making the very layered, multi-dimensional, deeper meanings and understandings of consciousness, self-mastery and awareness sound like it's a quickie recipe on the back of the Bisquick box.

I really wish people would post a great quote and then explore and/or explain their understanding of it. Open up the conversation. Allow for a discussion around what it means to you and then hear what others hear, experience, perceive when they read it.

If I had posted this meme I probably would have said something like: "The point of this quote isn't just that only you are responsible for your feelings, it's that you have the power to choose your feelings. And you also have the right to call out an asshole when they need to be called out. Be present to your feelings, be aware of them and understand from whence they came."

I recall a wonderful conversation with a great teacher I respect who said, "People are really bad communicators, and often their bad communication gets jumbled up with our terrible listening and chaos ensues. Hurt feelings, offense, arguments . . . shit just really goes downhill."

If I were to take this quote at face value (and I have), I would feel really bad most of the time. Why? Because it also implies that I should, to a certain degree, shut down my feelings. That I shouldn't feel the way I feel. I should not express my emotions or share them or in any way be vulnerable because no one cares. My feelings are my creation and my fault. Which means I no longer have the opportunity to truly value one of the greatest tool's humans have been given: the ability to feel.

For too long feelings and emotions have had a bad rap in the spiritual community. If I feel hurt, then I must have somehow created that reality so that I could learn some lesson about something that was "broken, wrong, or needed to be fixed" about me. And, for the record, let's be really clear here. I am partially responsible for the whole "You create your reality" hang up the whole New Age community has been ranting about for most of the new century.

As one of the creators of the film *What the Bleep Do We Know!?*, I have spent nearly 18 years explaining to people that it's hard to fully explore every detail of the concept "you create reality" in one movie. I've also realized that some of the inferences made in *What the Bleep* were too cute, glossed over, and over simplified. It's even caused many people to experience shame and guilt for having "created" certain events in their lives.

For that I am sorry. I was once a "newbie" and in many ways I still am. It took me a long time to let go of the notion that my actions have no impact and how others react to me is more about them than me— a notion that is actually quite dis-empowering.

The reality is, sometimes I am an asshole, a huge one. Mostly not intentionally. But still, it happens when I don't take the time to really understand that there are at least two people in an interaction and that we *both* have a responsibility to communicate consciously. When I fall back on the easy, "Hey, it's *your* problem you feel that way," I am not only NOT being conscious, I'm not truly living the full meaning of what I know the full depths of this quote is talking about: how to explore being present with our feelings and to master the art of our responses, reactions, awareness and our connection to how we feel, individually and together.

Unfortunately, not unlike what happened with the message "You Create Your Own Reality" in Bleep, too many people on the spiritual path have stopped at the easy part . . . at the obvious. And I don't mean just with this meme. And that's the purpose of this book. To examine quotes and concepts like this and explore them. To look into their deeper meaning and the before and after part as well.

Emotions are vital

It's not always about you. It's not always your feelings that are off base. Sometimes it's the person spewing meanness at you that has to take responsibility.

Feelings are not bad. They are a gift. No one should ever be made to feel guilty for having them. They are our guiding light. To make them wrong or bad or simply not our problem isn't fair to anyone. There is no spiritual growth in guilting one party and absolving another.

When we stop feeling, we stop living. Sure, it sounds great to live a life void of any emotional response to what is occurring around you. But, imagine not feeling the joy at the birth of a child, or love for another person, or the sweetness and connection after a great orgasm. Those cuddle hormones aren't being felt in a vacuum, just me, all by myself. I had help, and I'm really grateful for that help. I mean, I could do it alone. But experiencing it with someone else is way more pleasurable.

Our life's purpose and the spiritual journey are NOT about learning how to shut down our feelings, or to not engage them or to pretend that they don't exist. When I am hurt or mad or happy or excited or about to cum, you'll know! I will tell you. I will show you.

And I passionately believe that in that expression of my emotional response to you is an opportunity for growth for both you and for me.

For sure, having the ability to be aware of your feelings, aware not only of the feeling itself, but where it is manifesting from, i.e. is this feeling a response to an action from someone else that is pure, or have I tainted it with personal beliefs and crap that don't belong here? Have I listened honestly and without judgement? Did I muck it up with old fears and trauma? Or did this person intentionally set out to hurt me and cause me harm? Or did they do it unintentionally?

For a long time now, I have started to listen to not only the words being said, but the intention behind the words. I can always tell if the person I am in communication with is acting from their heart, or from their hurt. I can tell if they mean to cause me harm or are just really bad at saying what they want to say.

I ask questions. "Did you really mean to just call me a raging bitch or are you just angry and hurt and have no other way of expressing it? Why are you angry and hurt? Did I cause this or is something coming up for you that we can talk about?"

It's amazing what happens when you go beyond 280 characters. When you dig deeper into that meme or that feeling. This is why I've stopped posting quotables, especially ones with deep spiritual nuance and meaning. I am concerned that they do more harm than good. They begin to offer the opportunity for spiritual bypass.

I often hear my fellow-mom friends complain about how kids use LOL or TMI, as if language is dying out, and I laugh and wonder how many of us recently posted half a quote on FB just so we could sound enlightened.

My goal with this chapter and Cate's and my goal with this book isn't to call out any particular guru or teacher or to nitpick quotes. We are hoping that after reading this book we all will spend more time digging deeper into the meaning of familiar concepts and sayings, examining all the layers. We humans are multi-dimensional beings. We have many colors. Sometimes simplicity is good and sometimes it's an E-ticket to spiritual bypass.

P.S. - Post Consciously! That's my new motto. I have, in the past, posted quotes without taking the time to explore their meaning and nuances. Now? I'm putting myself on a meme diet.

Betsy Chasse is an award-winning filmmaker, best-selling author, change-maker, and mom. Best known as the co-writer, director and producer of the hit film *What The Bleep Do We Know?!*, Betsy has also produced the award-winning films Song of *The New Earth, Pregnant In America, Radical Dating* and *The Empty Womb*. She has authored multiple books including: *The Documentary Masterclass, Tipping Sacred Cows* and *What The Bleep Do We Know?!: Discovering The Endless Possibilities to Altering Your Everyday Reality*. In addition to co-publishing several best-selling collaborative books through her publishing company Rampant Feline Media, she also enjoys consulting with clients to develop multi-media content for world-wide distribution. For more information: www.Betsychasse.net

Chapter 2

I heard this expression early on in my spiritual quest. I didn't really understand how life could be an illusion, but for many years I took comfort in thinking that it was. So did a lot of my friends. For a long time it was kind of a running joke. But eventually I saw how I was using this metaphysical belief as a shield. If life wasn't really real, then I didn't have to take it seriously. And if I didn't take it seriously then maybe it couldn't hurt me as much. It took a long time to understand the deep mystical truth behind this saying, as well as all the BS around its literal interpretation and the damage that literalness perpetuates in the form of indifference and lack of engagement in vital global and environmental issues.

MARY CLARKE

LIFE IS AN ILLUSION

How many times have you heard somebody (some spiritual somebody) say, "Life is an illusion?" And have you noticed the only time anyone actually says this is when something bad has happened? Like your cat died and you're all teary and grieving. Or your major client went with another firm and you're pissed as hell. Or your car fell off the boat as it was being shipped to Honolulu. Or you're sitting in your living room, staring as this huge fatty lipoma that suddenly appeared on the outside of your thigh, ruining any thoughts about shorts and bathing suits on your upcoming vacation.

"Oh, well," your best friend (your spiritual best friend) says cheerily, poking at the fleshy protuberance. "You know what they say. It's all an illusion. Right?"

A little history

So where did this belief come from? In terms of New Age philosophy (which might as well be termed Old Age philosophy) the most direct source of this belief is from Vedanta, one of the six schools of Hindu philosophy dedicated to reflecting upon the information contained in the Vedas and the Upanishads. Vedanta philosophy uses the term "Maya" to sum up the cosmic illusion whereupon the One appears as many and the Absolute is experienced as the Relative in what we call this "reality."

Science has proven that all existence is a sea of undifferentiated energy. But all that energy shows up as a multifaceted, individualized and varied construct called "life." And because we depend upon our senses to perceive this world—especially our eyes which admit information in the form of a very narrow bandwidth of light into the brain—we see the diversity of life but not the deeper truth of its underlying unity. We see the form, not the energetic information behind the form. I see that "I" am over here and "you" are over there. When I dive into a swimming pool "I" don't merge with the water. I end up moving through it.

Does this mean the water is an illusion? No. It means the water *appears* separate from me—a situation expressed by the Austrian physicist Erwin Schröndinger when he called the world "schaumkommen," the world of appearances. The water is real. It just isn't fully seen because my limited, sense-based perceptions give me a limited view.

This is what Plato with his cave allegory was trying to get across. Basically we're all chained in a cave deep underground with our heads immobilized. We can't even look down and see our own bodies. A great fire burns behind us and our bodies cast shadows on the cave wall in front of us. Unable to perceive anything but the shadows, we mistake the shadows for reality.

And then there's the small fact that we don't even see things that are right in front of us.

Years ago I attended a conference where social anthropologist Dr. Marilyn Schlitz played a video of six people in an office hallway rapidly passing a volleyball around the group. Three of the players wore white shirts and three wore black shirts. She instructed the 60 people in the audience to count the number of times the ball was passed between the people wearing the white shirts.

About 20 seconds into the video I lost count and gave up the exercise. To my total shock, the moment I relaxed, a big guy in a gorilla suit suddenly materialized out of nowhere, standing in the center of the people passing the ball! He faced the camera, beat his chest, then turned and walked off camera while the ball exercise was still in motion.

"How many of you saw something unusual in this video?" Schlitz asked when the clip finished. One other woman and I raised our hands. The other 58 people saw nothing out of the ordinary. At that point she played the video again, instructing us to just "relax and sit there and watch." Audience reactions ranged from stunned to indignant, with a couple people accusing Schlitz of playing two different videos to trick them. But who needs somebody to trick us when we trick ourselves?

The whole point of the exercise was to show people how much information humans constantly miss—enormous things like a gorilla standing directly in front of a camera in a small hallway. Which made me rightfully wonder: What am I not seeing the rest of the time?

I don't have to be immobilized in a cave to miss what's going on. I miss what's going on walking and chewing gum on my way to the amusement park. But just because I don't see everything that's happening doesn't mean the world itself is an illusion.

Ramifications and a reassessment

In spiritual circles, the image of the lone ascetic in a cave in a loincloth, eyes closed in meditation, is iconic. And I spent decades with my own eyes closed focusing on "getting out of here." For me it was the whole point of meditation. Life was painful and confusing and the less I had to deal with it the better. And I was reassured in my uninvolved isolationist stance by hearing, over and over again, how "Life is an illusion" and "It's all Maya."

In the early years of my spiritual exploration I didn't have enough experience to understand how nuanced and layered these sayings were. I didn't know how multidimensional and subtle "reality" and perception are. In my youthful ignorance I very much took things at face value, these sayings among them. And I took great reassurance knowing this understanding came from ancient Hindu scriptures. A reliable source was telling me it was all make-believe! Yay!

Did I actually read the ancient scriptures and get some context? No. Did I study with a Vedic philosopher who could broaden my understanding? No. I read about Maya in some derivative New Age book somewhere and ran with it, greatly relieved I could retreat from the world and ignore the images of emaciated children in distant African nations, bellies bloated from starvation, flies crowding the corners of their eyes. I could throw out the pamphlets from various organizations struggling to save the dying oceans and plastic-choked whales, the burning rainforests and the starving polar bears.

"It's all just Maya," I would say with an airy wave of my fingers.

And then around 2006 Jesus got into the mix when I ran across *A Course in Miracles.* Not only did the Course tell me this world I lived in (and me with it) was an illusion, it informed me that nothing that ever happened in this world had ever really happened at all. Only God (Truth) is Absolute and therefore Real. And because God is Absolute, meaning whole and unchanging, anything that is relative, partial/separate and evolving/changing is not Absolute and therefore unreal. And because it is unreal it therefore doesn't exist. Never did exist.

Your mother may have just died in agony after a three-year battle with cancer. But don't worry. It never really happened.

The Course is purportedly the updated channeled teachings of Jesus, and who was I to argue with the words and insights of the Son of God? Never mind I and everybody else I met who read the Course were equally confused and head-scratching over the fact that Hiroshima and Vietnam, Michael Jackson and *Star Wars* never happened. Like me, they simply swallowed the teaching whole cloth, taking comfort in the fact that the world with all its pain and suffering was an illusion.

Whew! Thank you Jesus! I can conveniently turn my back on environmental issues, eroding women's rights, decaying ethical structures in government, ever-increasing health issues, drug and alcohol addiction and depression in the US, refusing to get involved.

I mean, what, after all, was there to get involved with?

It was finally the whole "It never happened" thing that jolted me from my slumber. I'm a logical woman. I can wrap my head around the fact that if there is no such thing as time, and only NOW, that all of Creation has already happened and was over and done with the very instant it was set into motion. I could "grok" that. But that Creation never happened at all? The Big Bang never happened? Universes and the cosmos weren't formed? Evolution never occurred? Human history never marched? I wasn't really here, thinking about all this shit?

Sorry. I don't buy it.

Mulling it over, I realized I'd had tons of experiences in altered consciousness over the years that clearly showed me that life, more than anything else, was dream-like. And looking at Creation as a dream helped me change my perspective. If life were a dream, the dream itself "happened." And zillions of people suffered horribly in the dream. *I* suffered in the dream. My now-deceased cat suffered in the dream. Millions of disappearing species suffered in the dream, teetering on the brink of extinction.

I took a harder look at metaphysical terminology and realized the words "Maya" and "schaumkommen" referred to *appearances*. The words meant things weren't as they seemed, not that all of life was an illusion. Eventually, I saw that the whole *Course in Miracles* spiel about the world not being real because it isn't Absolute and unchanging missed the whole point. The Course dismisses existence because it refuses to see the Absolute in existence itself. It focuses on the *appearances*, not the underlying unchanging divine substance of everything.

Finally, not even that mattered.

Screw spirituality and philosophy and metaphysics.

I woke up and decided that if life were a dream, I was damn well going to spend my time in it trying to ensure that the dream was a pleasant one for me and everyone and everything else instead of the nightmare it's fixing to become.

I got involved in politics, becoming a party delegate for Bernie Sanders in 2016. (*That* was an eye-opener!) I got involved in local environmental issues focused on getting rid of single-use plastic bags in stores and keeping oil refineries out of Puget Sound. I signed every freaking petition that crossed my desk from Change.org to the Environmental Working Group to the progressive branch of the Democratic party. And I gave money. And I gave my time.

I still do.

So what if life is an illusion? I'm apparently here. And while I am I want to be full-on *in*, not out.

Mary Clarke is a retired high school teacher and horse trainer. She still has quarter horses on her small ranch in northern Washington State, along with two Jersey cows, some goats, and three dogs. She still reads metaphysical self-help books and still meditates. She also enjoys writing and is working on a young adult novel about how human beings got lost when they developed egos, learning to separate themselves from the rest of Nature. Currently, she's gearing up to support Elizabeth Warren for president in 2020.

Chapter 3

Dedicate
your life
to perfection

122   2   2 Comments

Like   Comment   Share

Most religions hold up the icon of a perfected, enlightened being who transcended all human limitations while still living in a human body. Today in the West if a spiritual teacher has any human flaws they are judged as not knowing what they're teaching. As a result, so many people, especially spiritual teachers project this false image of: "Look at me! I'm basically perfect! Come learn from me so you that *you too* can become a perfected being!" I feel the belief in needing ourselves to be perfect (especially any spiritual teacher) places a huge, impossible-to-fulfill burden on everyone who is on the path of awakening, healing and transformation—especially those of us who answer the call from within to step into the teacher role and share our gifts with others.

Cameron Day

Perfection Is The Ultimate Goal

"Ego is Impurity. Be selfless. Consecrate and dedicate your life to perfection." This quote from spiritual teacher Frederick Lenz gives me chills because it points to the heart of everything I see as wrong with most ideas about what it means to be a spiritual person.

Ego is impurity? Maybe if you're talking about someone who doesn't have a healthy, integrated, well-functioning ego. Sure, that's most people, but I feel that obliterating the ego is not something that will serve most people very well in life. I'm going to skip the "be selfless," part, which would need a chapter (or a book) all of its own to point out why that's not a healthy way to live one's life, and get right to "… dedicate your life to perfection."

In my past, it has sounded really attractive to me to dedicate my life to perfection. My Goddess, if I could only be perfect, then everything in my life would be perfect. Right?

I have never known a perfect person, and I don't know what a perfect person would actually be like. I have heard a lot of ideas about how it would be if I were able to attain perfection: Always happy and positive, never sad or angry, having transcended "base human" impulses like sexual desire, being so "at one" with the universe that I feel constant bliss, knowing practically everything, being able to access mystical stores of universal knowledge to learn anything I don't yet know.

I would be able to thrive on a "perfect" vegan diet that did no harm to any living thing (except plants, but they don't have faces, so whatever). I would never desire alcohol or any chemical alteration of my physiology, and actually would have *no* desires whatsoever.

Right.

Perfect programming

As someone who has made a life's work as a spiritual teacher, (counselor, really), I have often wrestled with the notion that this career comes with an implied requirement to appear as perfect as possible to my clients and audience. I have endeavored to simply sit with the paradox that while I am a generally happy, well-grounded, positive-minded person, I don't fit *any* of the boxes of perfection, and yet I am able to help my clients gain deep self-insights and become more well-integrated people who naturally desire (desire!) to take care of their own needs while doing good for others.

Like many people, I grew up with Western and Eastern religious ideals of striving for perfection, like the perfect enlightenment of the Buddha(s), or the perfect selflessness of Jesus. I have also been saturated with the Western sociological and commercial ideals of perfection: I'm supposed to have perfect teeth, perfect skin, perfect hair, perfect posture, perfect clothing, perfect test scores, perfect academic achievement, perfect relationships, perfect physique, perfect business accomplishments, etc.

Perfection is a sneaky little infection. Almost none of the expectations of perfection I received from society and family were explicitly stated, but they were implied in a variety of ways: I should have done better in that class, should have scored higher on my SATs, should have "lived up to my potential" more highly, worked harder, done more, helped others more, given more, etc.

I resented and chafed against those expectations of perfection from family and teachers, rebelling by caring less and less about the external achievements that society lauded so highly, doing the least amount of work in order to accomplish those things. I was even reprimanded by a high school teacher for doing "just enough to get an A" in his class. I really didn't care. But underneath that "too cool for school" attitude, I struggled with feelings of not being enough. Not attractive enough, not accomplished enough, not fulfilling my potential enough, not being as kind as I could be, etc. When I refocused my energies on spiritual practices at age 21, I had all of these perfectionistic ideas in my subconscious mind which led me to superimpose them onto my spiritual aspirations.

I attempted to edit my thoughts and emotions so they would be "positive and enlightened," setting myself up to suppress "negative" emotions more intensely than I already had been. I meditated (of course), and learned methods of clearing negative emotions which were very effective, except for the fact that I approached them from the perspective of getting rid of things that were "imperfect" within myself, thus perpetuating the self-editing and suppression of those emotions.

I quickly learned energy clearing techniques, improvising and exploring new ways of using them from the very start of my training. I impressed the woman who was teaching me so much that we became partners, making a career out of helping people clear internal blockages and teaching our methods in workshops.

A bigger trap

In the course of this unusual career, I ran right into my wall of perfectionism. I believed that as a spiritual teacher I had to adhere to the ideals of perfection I ascribed to the enlightened teachers of the past. I also believed I must uphold the image of perfection that I could see and feel my students carried with them.

The problem, as I saw it, was that although I had deep spiritual insights, psychic awareness and the ability to catalyze massive internal shifts for clients, I wasn't living up to my ideas of a perfected spiritual person. I loved meat, wine and sex, but believed that I could only imbibe a well-moderated glass or two of wine over dinner with students from our workshops, explaining meat and wine consumption as a choice based in "spiritual awareness."

Finally, the inner dissonance became too much for me. I hated the feeling of being watched for any signs of having "clay feet" and disappointing the expectations of perfection from those who had come to learn from me. I eventually quit all teaching and session work so that I could focus on my own inner-work (and finally become perfect). It might sound like this was a terribly hard decision for me, but it was not. Instead, my sense of relief was profound. I could finally just be me, with all of my flaws, and I could stop trying to be so damn perfect.

In the following years I built a career as a freelance webmaster, channeling my perfectionism into computer code that could be objectively measured as "done right." I focused my inner work on shifting into acceptance and being fully present with an internal limitation without feeling the need to immediately clear it (aka get rid of the imperfection).

Sitting with flaws, limitations, emotional wounds and other undesirable internal conditions was very healing and illuminating for me. Through those long processes, I taught myself how to accept the parts of myself that I had been rejecting, and I learned to embrace the messy parts of myself that I had shoved down into the shadowy depths of my subconscious: Unworthiness, insecurity, shame, abandonment, heartache, fear, anger, resentment, sadness, depression, and others.

Through meditating on creative flow (messy) vs perfectionism (no mess allowed), I came to understand that the universe does not exist to be perfect, but rather as an artistic expression of consciousness that is completely allowed to be messy and perpetually unfinished. I learned to embrace the truth that all of my "bad" emotions are part of the tapestry of life, that they are "perfectly" normal parts of being a human. I still had a paradigm of clearing them away, but I had taken the major (and in hindsight, very obvious) step of sitting with them in acceptance before doing any clearing procedures.

A calling

Then one day something very unusual happened while I was meditating. A voice from deep within me rang out in my mind: "You have a gift. Share it."

Me: "Uh . . . I don't really want to do that. I'd rather just have more gifts."

Silence.

This is the only time in my life so far where what I call my Core Self (aka Higher Self) spoke in words directly to my conscious mind, and I really *really* didn't want to follow its suggestion. I was comfortably ensconced in my tech career and had no desire to step back into the role of a spiritual counselor and teacher.

Even though I had learned how to give myself permission to be as flawed as any other person while still working to better myself, I still didn't feel like I was "enough" for that path. My resistance no longer said that I wasn't "perfect enough," but it had plenty of other things to say: Not enlightened, not transcendent, and not psychic enough. I was still laboring with the beliefs that I needed to be more perfect in order to share my gifts with others. I wasn't even close to ready to go back into teaching—or so I thought.

Years of practicing self-acceptance had allowed my meditative experiences to expand dramatically, and I had developed an effective toolset for working in the energetic realm of human consciousness and the subconscious, including making peace with my ego instead of trying to annihilate it. The last thing I wanted to do was step into the role of spiritual teacher again, navigating those slippery slopes and ongoing expectations of perfection from myself and others.

And then life handed me a second prompt.

My grandmother had been in assisted care for almost a year, and her time was coming to a close. I told her to come to me when she died so I could help her transition. A few days later, I felt her presence and knew that it was time. I helped her release the guilt and shame that she had accumulated in this lifetime due to—you got it—the perfectionistic self-condemnation she had learned from her family of origin.

At the end of her release process, she was beaming with the light of her Core Self. Then it was an easy transition for her into a high-frequency realm of the non-physical universe that co-exists with our physical experience. Afterward, I felt immensely full of love and gratitude that doing this for another human being was even possible for me to conceive of much less actually accomplish. And I realized the gifts I have been given are too precious to only use for myself, family and friends.

A compromise

After accepting that it was time to share my gifts again, a whole new horizon of potential opened up to me. I decided that I would share the basics of what I knew for free via a website, charging to work one-on-one with clients, working remotely from my home in the woods of western Washington. I could teach classes online with the technologies that were emerging, circumventing workshops where people came from all over the country or world (as they had before) to hear me speak as if I had the answers to life's biggest questions.

I thought that I could avoid the "guru-trip" by not making my work about me at all, and simply be a soothing voice transmitting timeless wisdom on the internet. It worked for a while, until I started to gain a larger audience. With that popularity and increased demand for my session-work, the perfectionistic voices of my still-present inner-critic started to become more insistent: "You must do better, Cameron. You should be doing more. You're too relaxed, too lazy. You need to push yourself to attain higher levels of consciousness. You're not enough as you are. You *must* be better if you want to be successful, loved and admired. Never show your flaws or weakness. Nobody wants to hear about your limitations. They want help for their own issues. If you're in the midst of a struggle, you can't be a grounded anchor for your clients, so handle your issues on your own."

Self-talk like this was very difficult for me to confront because I still had a belief that being a spiritual person and especially a spiritual teacher meant that I needed to be striving for perfection, striving to be wholly focused on the well-being of others instead of myself. At the same time I also knew that in order to be "enlightened," happy and a force for good in the lives of others, I needed to free myself from the toxic bonds of perfectionist beliefs that were hiding in the shadows of my subconscious.

Through exploring my subconscious shadows, I realized I was equating vulnerability and revealing personal struggles with over-sharing the details of my life, violating my self-imposed rule, "Don't make your work about yourself." As I gently untangled the conflicting beliefs and motivations in my psyche, it became clear that my aloofness and hiding my weaknesses was yet another form of perfectionism. One of the key things I was seeking to avoid was right there, hiding in my shadow! Shit!

I was hiding behind a cloak of pseudo-perfectionism and succumbing to what I saw as one of the major pitfalls that befalls so many spiritual teachers: The belief that whispers, "Your audience want you to be perfect, so present yourself as such." Even the way I worked on myself and clients had a perfectionistic tint to it in the form of clearing away the imperfect parts of the psyche so that the (theoretically perfect) Core Self could be more fully embodied. The underlying message was that we are perfect at our core, so if we work hard enough and get clear enough, we can eventually become self-realized—basically perfect people.

As I unpacked the parts of my subconscious where old, perfectionisticbeliefs were entangled, I came to deeply understand that the most loving thing I could do for my clients *and* for myself was to embrace *all* the parts of my psyche and show them how to do the same.

Stretching the inner landscape

I learned to sit in a state of presence and acceptance for what is buried in my shadow instead of trying to clear it or release it or any other cleverly worded way to *get rid of that unwanted thing.*

I figured, "Well, this has been in my psyche, lurking in my subconscious for years, maybe even decades and it hasn't led to my ruin. So maybe I can just sit with it."

Well, that felt shitty, and it consumed *all* of my focus. So I learned to "stretch" my inner landscape and "hold a big space" so that instead of feeling like I was pressed up against an unsavory belief, emotion or self-judgment, I could sit in a large, warehouse-sized space with it.

In holding that big space, it became easier to stay grounded simply by feeling my legs and extending "energetic roots" from my feet into the earth. Super basic stuff, but I found those basics were easy to forget when I was smashed up against deeply-hidden beliefs that I wasn't worthy of being loved, and that all of my relationships would end with abandonment, or maybe something less intense, like I wasn't really as smart or evolved as I liked to believe.

I learned to say, "Yes, AND…" to those beliefs and self-judgments. To say to them, "That might be true, AND there might be more to the story. Yes, I feel unworthy of love right now, AND maybe I am just as worthy as love as anyone else, even with all of my flaws."

I made a daily practice out of holding self-judgmental thoughts in a big space, saying to them and myself, "Yes, and…" while remaining grounded and present with that internal content. Through this process, I gradually became more relaxed and loving toward myself and more loving and relaxed with clients, friends and family, even when they were in crisis. I could hold a big space for what IS to such a degree that nothing seemed overwhelming. And that's a big "wow."

Through freeing myself from beliefs that I needed to be perfect, I was able to deeply embody authentic self-love that is subtle, gentle and very relaxed. I learned that being relaxed with myself and with others is one of the most loving things I can do for me or for another person.

Self-love and self-acceptance is relaxing. Perfectionism creates tension. A lot of tension.

Perfectionism says, "Oh shit! I made a mistake! Fix it quick before someone rejects me!" Spiritual perfectionism says, "Oh shit! I made a mistake! Fix it quick before God rejects me!"

On the other hand, self-love says, "Oh look, I made a mistake. That's going to take some time to fix, but I'll probably learn a lot from this experience."

I learned that self-acceptance leaks out into our interactions and relationships, transmitting a subtle message that says, "Everything is going to be all right. I love myself enough to love you just as you are, with all of your flaws, which are no worse than my flaws. Things are going to get better as we both love ourselves into greater levels of wholeness."

So if you notice you have been hiding parts of yourself, trying to present a perfectly happy face at the expense of authentically expressing your feelings and desires, I want you to know there are more self-loving options available. Try holding a big space of acceptance for what you are feeling, your resistance to the feelings, your fears, hopes and desires.

Do your best to accept every single thing connected to that feeling. No other techniques, just acceptance of everything that you are holding in the biggest inner-space possible.

With enough self-loving acceptance, you can rise above the self-suppression of perfectionism and express exactly who you are and what you feel from moment to moment. And it will be the best gift you ever gave others *and* yourself.

Cameron Day - As a spiritual counselor and teacher, Cameron Day has been sharing his iconoclastic perspectives on what it means to be an embodied, integrated, spiritual human being for over 20 years. His focus on deep, self-loving acceptance and being fully present with what IS, rather than fighting against what feels undesirable within a person or in their lives sets his work apart from modalities that promise eventual perfection. He has worked one-on-one with hundreds of clients through thousands of sessions, and his primary focus is teaching classes online to a global audience via his websites such as www.ManifestClearly.com and www.AscensionHelp.com. His next online class, scheduled to be taught in winter of 2019, can be found at www.LovingWholeness.com, where he will teach simple, powerful techniques for accepting every part of a person's self and integrating the deeply shadowed parts of our subconscious that most methodologies do not address.

Chapter 4

I love the idea that "everything is love" and how the utopian community seems to be a manifestation of that ideal. (My soul mission is to restore Heaven on Earth). But I think most people have misguided thinking when it comes to both love and what it takes to live in sustainable community. Most of us can't even live sustainably *outside* of community. It sounds wonderful in theory, but I think the reason we don't have many working models is that eventually these communities disband because things didn't work out. Perhaps many of us have come from planets or other dimensions where we did interact from a place of "Everything is love" and we want to replicate that here on earth? Unfortunately, most people don't seem ready to take responsibility and do the grunt work necessary to make this happen here. Love isn't easy and there are no free rides, even though utopia sounds like one!

SUSIE BEILER

EVERYTHING IS LOVE

One of the outcomes of the whole "All you need is love" or "Everything is love" concept that's so pervasive in the spirituality community is the belief in the ideal of utopian communities where people come together and live in productive, peaceful, loving harmony. Or, perhaps, the "Everything is love" idea came out of the old school attempts at utopia and the "Love Not War" movement of the hippie era in the 1960s. Either way, I happen to *not* believe that everything is love, practically speaking. Nor do I believe that the majority of humanity, even the majority of the spiritual community, is ready to build utopia.

My cultural lineages are Amish and Mennonite. My grandfathers were both born into the Amish church and I grew up in a fairly conservative Mennonite home where modesty and obedience were the rule of the day. The three basic tenets of Mennonites are 1) living a simple life, 2) being of service, and 3) pacifism—great utopian ideals. Many of these conservative communities have a deep history of working and living together. An Amish barn-raising is the quintessential example of unity in action. The women prepare food while the men work together to erect the barn. From an outside perspective these communities can appear to be demonstrating spiritual ideals of what it truly means when someone says, "The world is made of love," or "It's all love." Everyone plays their role harmoniously and it's all peachy keen, at least at the surface.

Yet even Amish communities scream "shadow" when you consider the spiritual oppression prevalent in their churches. There is so much judgment and control exercised by the bishops and those in leadership. One must abide by very strict rules that limit freedom and self-expression. For example, if your child is kicked out of the church, they are not allowed to come back home and you as the parent are not supposed to talk with them or see them ever again. As a church member, you must abide by a strict dress code. Your words must be chosen carefully, and you must follow the Bible as your rulebook for life. There is no exploration of who you are as a divine being or what you might have to offer from this perspective. If it's not in the Bible or approved by the bishop, you don't have the chance to experience it.

I was very sheltered until I left college. I wasn't taught how to stand up for myself. ("The meek shall inherit the earth.") I did not know, for example, that living only in service isn't balanced. I was constantly giving of myself and didn't take time to care for my own needs, or even acknowledge that I had needs. I didn't understand the Law of Circulation, so I was like a one-way valve, only giving and rarely receiving. Later, in my career as a Pediatric Occupational Therapist, I was driving around the city all day seeing patients and educating parents. I cared so deeply for each family, once I left the homes of my patients, I didn't know how to detach from them and I would energetically carry them with me. I did not know about healthy boundaries and letting go. Subconsciously, I thought I was responsible for their progress.

On some level I thought that taking care of the needs of others would take care of my needs. I didn't realize that I needed to do things to nurture myself such as taking walks in nature and spending time with friends. Honestly, at that time, I didn't even know what I liked or what would nourish me. I wasn't taught to get to know myself. I was only ever taught to serve others.

An awakening

In my early twenties, I suffered from Chronic Fatigue Syndrome (CFS). Only then did I begin to understand that I was lacking balance and boundaries. I had given too much of myself and was severely lacking in the self-care department!

After a great deal of time and attention to self-care, I was on the acupuncture table in December of 2004, when I suddenly *knew* that I no longer had CFS. It was truly a "lightbulb moment" where every cell in my body changed and I knew I was fully healed. I had the "I am God" moment and found my own divinity within. In the following months and years, I worked to deconstruct all the programming of the church and society. I also adopted new belief systems that reflected my healing experiences. I found metaphysical groups and churches and interacted with people who shared their ideas about how life could be different on this planet. Since my sudden spiritual awakening, I've heard many people discuss utopian ideals of intentional communities where all people come together to live and work in harmony and, to be honest, I've had these dreams myself. But what I've realized as I've gotten to know myself better, is that, for the most part, people aren't ready for this, myself included. Allow me to explain.

I am an ultra-sensitive empath. And I would absolutely love to live and work with balanced, integrated people with coherent brains, consistent work ethics and logical needs and the capacity for self-responsibility. My idea of heaven on earth includes being around humans who are highly functional in their abilities to healthily flow their emotions, address community concerns rationally and with neutrality, bring brilliant ideas to the table, evolve humanity together … you see where I'm going with this. But let's get real for a second. How many people do you know who can effectively deal with their triggers (emotional charges) in the moment? How many people have you met who know how to maintain dynamic balance? I'll put it more simply. How many people do you want to hang out with 24/7, 365 days a year, for a lifetime in close proximity?

You don't have to be an empath for people to wear on you. And, if you're sensitive like me, you can only handle other energies a little bit at a time. With the current state of rapid change and imbalance on our planet, I can't imagine coming together in a living situation with a bunch of people who don't have deep skills of self-awareness and self-healing. Yes, I believe we all did come to this planet to work together and create something new and better together. But we don't have to live together to create together.

Striving for unity amidst duality

The overall perspective of life on planet Earth is that we are navigating a polarized reality. According to those that believe in this experience, the first "things" created after the Big Bang were positrons and electrons, in other words, opposing positive and negative electromagnetic charges. Electromagnetic polarity is what this reality is based upon. This means that wherever we go, whatever we do, we encounter the light *and* the shadow, the good and the bad, the right and the wrong, the pleasant and the unpleasant. The two always show up together in some way. This means that anyone living in a communal environment is constantly dealing with both the positive and negative sides of themselves and everyone else all the time!

This is just life. And this is fine … as long as people are consciously dealing with it. It's up to us to exercise discernment as to what is truly of the light and what is of the shadow, then own it, process it and go beyond it. And yet most people, in my opinion, don't do this.

Have you ever met a "spiritual person" who seemed too good to be true? They were polished and smiling and always happy … and then you saw the not-so-nice side they tried to keep hidden? Suddenly you wanted to run away from the monster they became before your very eyes! Living in the spiritual Mecca of Sedona, Arizona, I have known many individuals like this. When I first met them, they were all love.

They were overly happy and everything was always great. But when the shit hit the fan and they had to face themselves, they either moved toward psychosis or they entered a crisis because they couldn't face their shadow. The once loving, carefree person suddenly yells and screams, seemingly with no context because something didn't go their way. I'm sure you can think of an example of someone like this in your own life.

On the other hand, what if that person was integrated with the shadow part of themselves? They would appear more real to you. You would be able to feel their authenticity. They would be equally comfortable expressing themselves on a good or bad day in a way that they weren't projecting their crap onto you. This is an example of an integrated person. They're real and raw, yet balanced. There is no hiding or attempt to hide any part of themselves. The shadow aspect of themselves is integrated because it's accepted without judgment. I have several friends like this. We share openly and vulnerably with each other. When times feel rough, we don't hide what's going on, but we seek help from each other and hold space for each other to vent, to cry, to scream, or whatever is needed in the moment.

Now be real with me. How many people do you know like this? Not so many right? So, can you imagine living with ten or 15 or 30 people in a community and the majority had never faced their shadow? Couldn't face their shadow? And instead go around projecting all their crap onto the people around them while talking about how "Everything is love?" What business do we have saying that everything is love when we haven't transmuted our meanness and insecurity, our jealousies and hatreds? How do we honestly think we can create utopian societies when most people on the planet do not have the basic fundamental skills to even *see* let alone integrate their shadow aspects?

Does this mean we shouldn't try to come together to create our utopian societies? Of course not. But from a purely realistic perspective, in order for these things to work, we need to be more practical and less idealistic. From the everyday perspective of most people running around with un-integrated shadows, many taking medications just to get by, clearly everything is *not* love, no matter how much we wish it were or how often we proclaim it. We have a lot of work to do on ourselves before we can create something sustainable and loving together.

Getting it together

I have several significant communities in my life that guide my thinking, my inner circle of friends, my Creation Temple community (an online membership website with weekly video gatherings), and my family. My experience in creating and sustaining community tells me that before genuine utopia can unfold on this planet, before we can create a world where "All is love," that we all need to be comfortable with transparency, allowing our deepest darkest secrets to come into the light. We need to learn the skills of communication without blame and judgment. We need to be willing to take risks and "put it all out there," laying our lives on the line for change. We need to step up and take full responsibility for all that we've created so far and what we are currently creating. We need to be real, honest, and learn how to be deeply vulnerable. We need to cultivate safety within ourselves, healing our cellular trauma from brutal deaths and failures when we tried to do this in other lifetimes. We need to forgive ourselves for how we have failed this lifetime. We need to remember our power, our wholeness, our souls!

In this moment, I invite you to do some self-reflection. Are you ready to live like everything is love and love is all there is? If you really believed this, what would change in your life? How would your relationships change? Would your career change? Would you really be spending your time in the same way you do currently?

Look at your communication skills. Are you honest with yourself and others? Do you keep your word? Do you speak honestly and forthrightly or are you passive aggressive or even silent about matters that deserve your voice? Do you know when to share your voice and when to just listen? Do you dominate conversations or are you the quiet "mouse in the corner" who has great wisdom but doesn't offer it unless asked? In cooperative systems all voices need to be heard. All opinions and inspirations need to be aired. Yes, there can be a council where elders come together and also hear the voices of the young, but the totality of voices needs to be considered.

And then there's self-love. If you want to experience utopia, you must first practice honoring yourself. Set healthy boundaries. Nourish your spirit and feed your body well. Hydrate. Commune with nature. Move to the rhythms of your body and circulate your flow. Be true to yourself. Take time out to nurture your soul. Listen to and honor your heart's desires. Appreciate all parts of yourself.

Have you healed your inner child or are you at least in the process of healing him/her? Do you even know who or what your inner child is? In order to live peacefully among each other we must know how to deal with triggers and wounds. None among us is perfect. We all have hurts from the past that haunt us, unless we have and use the proper tools for self-healing. It starts with self-awareness and the ability to be honest with ourselves and confront what wants to be healed and integrated.

Once we make progress with self-healing, only then can we consider coming together in intimate community. The people around you are your mirrors. They reflect to you your strengths as well as your shortcomings. Living in close community will bring triggers. It will bring up your wounds, your expectations, judgments, and preconceived notions. And if you don't have some foundational skills for what to do when this happens, it can quickly become overwhelming to face the "mirror" that is your community.

Another thing to consider is if other community members as equally invested as you are and willing to work through any potential issues? What do you know about these people? How long have your known them? Do they have a solid background that would lend towards making them beneficial community members? Your utopian society will only be as strong as its weakest member. It only takes one saboteur to ruin the whole thing. Do you have what it takes to withstand the trials that are sure to surface? These are things you'll want to consider before jumping in. Proceed with great discernment.

Sustainable change takes effort and time. Most people simply aren't willing to invest in transforming themselves to the point where they would be a good candidate for a spiritual community where they live and work side-by-side with others. I'm 14 years deep into my spiritual path, consistently rebirthing myself into better, more integrated versions of me, and I *still* wouldn't consider myself a good candidate for an eco-community, at least, not the kind where we live in close proximity, interacting every day.

Is heaven on earth possible? We have a long way to go, and yet, I do remain hopeful.

Many miracles and blessings have unfolded in my own life when I've stepped up to take responsibility for my creations, so I do believe in a harmonious future. But it will take work. It will take personal integration as well as collective cooperation. From a spiritual perspective, we are at a tipping point on this planet and the masters that have paved the way for us have left us energy templates, tools, and wisdom that can accelerate the process. Those awakening now are quickly accessing their true selves at greater speeds than those who awakened 30 years ago. The energy is supporting this. I know that we as human race can do this. Utopia, here we come!

Susie Beiler is a Certified Holistic Health Practitioner and the founder of The Creation Temple®, an online resource for supporting Lightworkers in their spiritual path. With training in Occupational Therapy and Holistic Nutrition, Susie experienced a profound shift in 2004, after a sudden spiritual awakening. She healed herself from Chronic Fatigue Syndrome (adrenal burnout) and began a new path devoted to her inner work, healing and reprogramming her brain in profound ways. In 2014, Susie took a leap of faith when she left Pennsylvania not knowing where Spirit was guiding her. Now, she's a channel for the divine, a Facilitator of Sacred Ceremony, and a Master of the Healing Arts. Susie utilizes a variety of modalities including DidgeriDeep Sound Healing™, Holistic Nutrition, Spiritual Guidance & Lifestyle Coaching, DNA Activations, and Energy Healing. She works with deeply sensitive empaths to tap into their divine power, master their energy, and live their soul mission. Susie is a dynamic public speaker with a commanding stage presence. She lives and leads retreats in Sedona, AZ and enjoys nature, authenticity, and high vibrational food. For more information:

www.susiebeiler.com and www.creationtemple.com

Chapter 5

I thought that *seeking* was the answer to everything, from eliminating cancer to becoming more spiritually connected to manifesting my desires, and even healing others. A notion attributed to Jesus and made widespread in the Christian church for hundreds of years, it was popularized within the New Age movement over the last several decades. Nowadays this saying is so often about getting what we want—from spiritual enlightenment to a million dollars—encouraging us to myopically focus on our end goal, strive to get there, use the right techniques etc. We wear the phrase "spiritual seeker" as a badge of honor, setting us apart from the rest of the world and communicating to the universe, "Bring it on!" But more than anything it seems what's been brought on is a lot of ego-led striving getting in the way of receiving, separating spirituality from the rest of life.

CHRISTINE UPCHURCH

THE DOWNSIDE TO SEEKING

If you're on your conscious path, you may consider yourself to be a "spiritual seeker." Google those two words together and you will come up with literally millions of results—a cornucopia of blogs, articles, websites, books, and workshops. The spiritual journey popularized by the New Age movement has been going strong for the last several decades. It certainly can be transformative to consciously connect with our spiritual nature and look for ways to nurture that connection. But dare I say it? There can be *downsides* to seeking.

If you've only recently begun your conscious journey, I apologize for offering you some true but very disappointing news: this journey is rarely easy. For those of you who are veterans of this path, hearing "easy" and "spiritual path" in the same sentence might lead you to groan, curse, or burst out laughing because *you know better.* Sometimes the soul may dangle the proverbial carrot of inner peace to lead us forward, and it is oh-so-tempting to follow. For many of us, it is so compelling that we have no other choice. What we often don't realize is that what lies ahead can become a circuitous journey including potholes, unprecedented storms, and only glimpses of that promised land.

Fitting in

Looking back at my childhood, I think I was very connected to the spiritual realm from a very young age. For instance, I was fairly intuitive and sometimes knew what others were thinking or feeling before they expressed it. I sensed that my natural state somehow included an ability to float freely from one place to another, and I found it confusing that I could only manage to do it while sleeping. I also recall feeling connected to animals and insects (yes, even the dangerous ones!), and I was particularly fascinated by the light which I sometimes saw emanating from them.

Strangely, I don't recall seeing light around most people in the same way. Yes, I saw good in people and felt love from certain family members, friends, and teachers. However, I sometimes felt uneasy around people as they seemed prone to anger abruptly, to blame and shame others, or to demonstrate disregard for the life of the very animals and insects I so loved. I came to understand that this place called Earth is a strange mix of vibrant light and dysfunctional darkness, having a deep knowingness that the darkness is not our natural state. I did my best to fit in, sensing that there is another place more comfortable and loving than this one. But I also realized that I am in human form for an important purpose, serving my own growth as well as that of the collective.

As I entered into adulthood, I followed what I thought was a sensible path, choosing a career direction which I believed would ultimately lead me to financial success, societal respect, and a "normal" life. Near the end of my undergraduate studies in mathematics, I was trying to decide whether to go into computer science or attend graduate school to study statistics. Twice during this decision period I heard an odd, disembodied voice speak to me with a loud and emphatic urging: "You're a healer!" I was shocked by the absurdity of hearing such a voice as well as by its message.

Initially, I focused on the fact that I heard that voice—a voice which not only sounded very different than my typical mind chatter, but also seemed to have come from outside of me *even though no one else was around*. After setting aside my astonishment, I began to ponder the voice's message. What would it mean to be a healer? At that stage of my life I believed that a healer must be close to perfect, always filled with joy and love. That certainly didn't describe me. At that time, I was smothered by unworthiness, striving to prove myself worthy via continual perfectionism. I felt an uneasy burden resulting from a childhood trauma that I was not yet equipped to face—an incident of molestation at age five, still buried deep within my memory. Despite the fact that our relationship was often tumultuous, I had recently become engaged to my childhood sweetheart. I was also pursuing a career which I was well equipped to handle but which wasn't connected to my heart.

After pondering the enormity of what it might mean to be a healer—juxtaposed with the awareness of the heavy emotional baggage I was carrying—I concluded that this "idea" was the most egotistical thing my mind had ever created. Consequently, I confused the soul's voice-on-megaphone for the voice of ego and ignored the message about being a healer. Instead, I plunged ahead with my so-called sensible direction.

Wake-up call

One of the things I've learned on my path is that when your soul is calling and you ignore it, life takes you on a detour to bring you face-to-face with an oversized, illuminated billboard displaying its message. When I ignored the communication about being a healer, life ultimately challenged me to face it. While working as a statistician and doing research for my doctoral dissertation in mathematical statistics, I developed the early stages of lymphoma. As life would have it, early treatment for this type of cancer was inadvisable. The medical plan was to wait until the disease progressed enough and then begin weekly chemotherapy—*and remain on it for the rest of my life*. While my symptoms were mild, facing this potential future was devastating. I fell into an emotional and spiritual abyss, longing for a soft place to land. But there was no such place.

If I were to identify a moment in my life when I began to *seek* in earnest, it was sometime in the first few weeks following this diagnosis. Feeling quite alone in my health challenge, I felt compelled to try to connect with something that might bring me solace. Feeling betrayed by my body, I sought validation that there might be some sort of divine purpose underlying my situation. Feeling disempowered by lack of treatment options, I sought approaches that might lead me to a miracle. I learned to meditate, did affirmations, and visualized my wellbeing. I changed my diet, went on a yoga retreat, and read every book on healing I could find. I also went into therapy to lighten that load of emotional baggage.

In order to heal, I did my best to think positive thoughts. I ate the "right" diet. I attempted to release negativity stored in my body via yoga. I used manifestation techniques daily. I paid lip service to the idea that this life detour was serving an important purpose, even though I was struggling to understand the "big why" of my illness. Yet despite all my effort, the cancer progressed anyway. Then one day I stepped away from the New Age packaging of my health crisis and consciously acknowledged how powerless I felt. Instead of feigning positivity and avoiding the depth of my darkness, I swam *into* it. I began to cry in despair. The crying turned into sobbing, followed by more sobbing, until finally I surrendered into complete exhaustion. Strangely, it was then that I heard the voice again. It said, "*Now* we can work together."

From that moment of really letting go, I became more energized and felt more empowered. I had greater ease and became more adept at redirecting my choices according to intuitive guidance. Following that inner guidance was sometimes rather easy, such as becoming less restrictive with my diet. After recognizing that the *fear* associated with eating the "wrong" food was far more toxic than the food itself, I allowed myself to eat whatever felt right—even when it was an occasional, decadent treat geared toward satisfying my inner child.

Other times, following that internal guidance led to greater upheaval in my life. For example, when I was only months away from completing my Ph.D., I chose to leave my doctoral program which wasn't bringing me joy, and then move across the country to an area that felt more supportive of my health. Navigating in this new way wasn't always easy. It required that I let go of some of my pre-programmed "shoulds" and maintain a more neutral sense of curiosity about what was actually right for me. Then I had to follow through by acting upon that guidance, even when it felt difficult or didn't seem "sensible." Ultimately, I got my miracle: the cancer disappeared without any medical treatment.

Reorientation

Experiencing that healing was thrilling, but it was also rather perplexing to my scientific mind. I moved forward from that empowering life lesson with a thirst for knowledge about the mind-body connection, energy healing, and conscious manifestation. Eventually I stepped into the role of healer, just as that voice had prompted me to do so many years earlier.

For a long time, I thought that in order to achieve a particular outcome (health or otherwise), it was imperative that a person seek it with myopic focus while holding the "right" beliefs and doing the "right" manifestation techniques. Yet that theory got turned upside down within the context of my healing practice. As a healer, I came to understand that the best I could offer my client was to let go of any attachment to outcome and approach the session from a place of curiosity about what wanted to shift. I had clients who didn't believe in my work and didn't believe they could heal, and yet they healed anyway, sometimes very quickly. I also had clients who were doing all the "right" things who didn't heal. In some sense, my clients' seeking, or lack thereof, didn't seem to correlate with the outcome.

Although so much of it remains a mystery to me, one thing paradoxically feels true: The vibration of surrender—which some may argue is the opposite of seeking—seems to fuel our forward movement toward positive change, whether that change is an outcome we consciously desire or a wonderful soul-surprise. Just as it was with my healing from cancer, letting go is often essential. If we strive or struggle when seeking what we want, then we can get in the way of receiving it.

If seeking a particular outcome that we want to manifest can have its downsides, then what about seeking a spiritual connection? On one level, I understand the desire to connect with something more, to become more "enlightened," or to find more inner peace. I have no regrets about choosing to approach life with greater consciousness. But I have gotten to a place in life where I am beginning to question the wisdom of *seeking*—or at least how I go about it. Afterall, my connection was there as a child. If I am seeking, doesn't that imply that somehow it has gotten lost and needs to be found from its hiding place? Doesn't that mean that I don't trust that I will experience it unless I *do* something? And who is it leading that search—my spirit or my ego?

We are born whole, with both a connection to our spiritual nature as well as to our five senses. I find it interesting that we can become obsessive about seeking to experience the spiritual, but we generally don't do that with the physical. Imagine how strange it would be if we thought we needed to strive to experience taste. Instead, we take it for granted as being a part of who we are. Might we have more to learn about the nuances of taste, say, relating to wine? Sure. But it wouldn't keep us from enjoying a glass of wine with our dinner before we got around to taking that wine tasting class!

I have found it helpful to stop compartmentalizing my spirituality as though it is separate from my mental, emotional, and physical experiences. When I trust that it is already there as a given part of my wholeness—continually intermingling with every other aspect of my being—then I experience life much more expansively. This suggests that perhaps my many years of seeking spirituality may have often been getting in the way of experiencing it!

Once I came to terms with the fact that there can be downsides to seeking, I found myself struggling to reconcile this awareness with the Bible phrase, "Seek and ye shall find." In some ways I still found it to be a powerful message. But was there something I was missing about it? After doing some research, I discovered something fascinating. When this phrase from the New Testament was translated from Greek into English, it was mistranslated! Instead of "Seek and ye shall find" it should have been "Keep on seeking and ye shall find." Specifically, the true translation doesn't mean "keep on" as in over and over again, but rather "keep on" continuously, as in *all the time*. This subtle difference in translation significantly changes its meaning and how we might apply that wisdom in our daily lives.

I don't think that this revised translation means that we should be spending every moment thinking, "I want *this!*" or "I need *that!*" as though the universe needs us to continuously bombard it with our intention in order to help us manifest it. Rather, I believe the true translation suggests our focus should be less on achieving a particular goal and more about always being aware and open to receiving. So instead of focusing on wanting *that* relationship when feeling ready for love, we could look for signs and circumstances which lead us to that next right relationship, with ease and in perfect timing. Instead of focusing on our desire to have *that* job at *that* amount of money, we could instead focus on sharing our gifts while being supported, then watching what unfolds as we courageously step forward. Instead of seeking to experience certain spiritual "bells and whistles," we could instead embrace all of who we are and then observe how that, in turn, expands our spiritual connection.

I now understand that seeking can have its downsides, including having attachment to the "right" path, egoically investing in "doing" rather than "being," dysfunctionally compartmentalizing our wholeness, and undermining the trust required to fully let go. Despite the potential downsides, I continue to seek in my own way—partly because I see there can be upsides and partly because it seems to be intrinsic to who I am. Yet I have become more mindful of how I go about it. Applying the wisdom from the corrected translation of that Bible phrase, I now choose to seek in a new way. I am letting go of the habit of seeking the way a hunter would use narrow-minded determination to go after a buffalo. Rather I now choose to seek more like a gatherer, maintaining a wider focus and being open to whatever is along my path.

This doesn't mean that I never seek something specific. Just like a gatherer might want berries and have a keen sense about the appropriate timing to search for them, I too may choose to seek something when it feels right. It might be something as mundane as asking for inner guidance so that I can find my way to a good Mexican restaurant when traveling. It also might be something more significant, such as looking to manifest the right business support for bringing my wisdom to the world. I have found that when I do seek something specific, sometimes I get exactly what I want, and sometimes I don't. And sometimes what I receive is even better than what I initially set out to find.

Taking this new approach is helping me to avoid some of the potential downsides of seeking. It has also been transformative because it is making me more open to all of life—learning to trust that there will be varied and abundant sustenance along my journey.

Christine Upchurch, MS is an award-winning leader, writer, TEDx speaker, workshop leader, spiritual myth buster, healer, Vibration of Change™ creator and coach, and host of the nationally syndicated *The Christine Upchurch Show* now in its seventh year. She has been a featured guest on radio shows across North America and has taught thousands around the globe. Christine, who has been called "the best radio host ever," also supports authors and entrepreneurs in getting their messages out more successfully through one-on-one coaching as well as with her program *Become a Best Guest: How to Interview More Effectively on Radio and Podcasts.* Christine is the author of the upcoming book entitled *The Top 20 Myths about Spirituality,* which challenges some of the well-established beliefs within the consciousness community so that we can "get real" about our spiritual nature. She is passionate about helping people to shift their perspective so that they can embrace a more expansive way of living. Author and legendary human potential leader Dr. Jean Houston calls Christine "a midwife of souls." For more information: ChristineUpchurch.com or Top20Myths.com

Chapter 6

Detachment is such a spiritual buzz word. Thing is, there are so many different ways to understand that one word—so many nuances and layers! I've seen a lot of people, myself included, get hung up on understanding what detachment is and applying it. Instead of being an inspiring goal and practice, it all too often becomes this heavy New Age "have to" that ends up being more about avoidance and apathy than anything else. And the last thing we need in this world right now is apathy and more spiritual by-passing.

KATHERINE ELLIS

THE MYTH OF DETACHMENT

The concept of detachment was one of the very first aphorisms I picked up as I entered the spiritual arena. Perhaps this was because I became interested in spirituality hard on the heels of a very painful divorce from the man I'd considered for years to be "the love of my life."

All things eventually fade in this Earthly reality—flowers, youth, fame, relationships, and all too often love itself. I think realizing this at age 30 was one of the reasons detachment seemed so attractive to me. It seemed to be the key to avoiding heartache, disappointment and any other type of emotional suffering I might encounter along the rest of my life's path. If I kept myself from getting deeply involved with people or situations, from lovers and business partners to good causes like volunteering at the local animal shelter—if I kept myself wrapped in aloof detachment, how could I possibly get hurt again?

I even hung the Indian sage Sri Chinmoy's pithy saying on a wall in my condo's hallway: "Your heart must become a sea of love. Your mind must become a river of detachment." I wasn't sure how to experience both love and detachment at the same time. In fact, I rather thought they were mutually exclusive territories. But surely Sri Chinmoy, a yogi, spiritual master and a life-long unmarried celibate, knew what he was talking about?

Getting serious about spirituality

I must have passed that saying 10,000 times as I went in and out the front door, going about working as a real estate agent in the beautiful historic city of Charleston, South Carolina. But, as the years passed, I gradually forgot about the first half of the saying, focusing more and more on the detachment part as I forged my way through life.

Eventually I found myself in a long-term love affair with a married man who assured me he and his wife had an arrangement of "don't ask, don't tell." How much more safely detached could I get?

Not surprisingly, I found myself getting more satisfaction out of my spiritual practices of daily yoga and meditation than I did any engagements in the outside world. In fact, my life rapidly took on a kind of strange division. None of my friends at the office shared my interest in spiritual matters. My lover didn't either. In fact, being an atheist, he found it curiously quixotic—something he tolerated with mild amusement but certainly did not respect. As a result, the outside part of me that did what it took to stay afloat economically, maintain friendships and business relationships and some semblance of a love life seemed to grow more distant from the inside part of me. I lived for the quiet hours after work at home where I could read spiritual self-help books and meditate. And even though being a real estate agent meant that it was in my best interests to be available to the outside world (at least by phone) at ungodly hours of the day and night, seven days a week, I started disconnecting my phone line after 8 pm, refusing to turn it back on until 9 a.m.. And Sundays I devoted to my meditation practice.

I joined a spiritual school that advocated long hours of sadhana, abstinence from alcohol and abstinence from sex. I managed the meditation and no alcohol, but couldn't quite wrap my brain around the no sex part! I remember sitting in a vast lecture hall with perhaps 300 other students, back ramrod straight, all of us sitting in lotus posture for hours on end (tortured hours for me!), unmoving, listening to our "master teacher" lecture about the need for mental discipline, emotional detachment and rigorous focused intention upon the end goal of enlightenment which would, he assured us, be worth all the hard work and dedication on our part.

Often we would be asked to share personal information during classes about our struggles with daily existence with our "partner" (whoever was sitting next to us on the right, or sometimes a small group of fellow students sitting together). I remember being particularly impressed with one man I sat next to during a week-long retreat one summer. We had assigned seating that had to be maintained throughout the entire retreat, and he was unflinching in maintaining his lotus posture, even during lectures that went on for more than four hours. When it came time for us to share, turns out he was in the middle of a messy divorce from his wife. The reason? The no sex rule. (The rule I was so blithely ignoring.)

"Ve already haf four children," he said in impeccable yet heavily Norwegian-accented English. He shrugged his skinny shoulders, his white-streaked untrimmed beard flowing down across his chest. "I haf gone beyond such vorldly distractions and no longer haf the need for such base animal expression." His mouth twisted with distaste.

"But don't you love your wife and children?" I asked, somewhat shocked. "Do you have to split up over this? Won't you miss them?"

He shrugged again, his indifference palpable. "Vat is, is. Eff she cannot support me in my spiritual goals that is her problem. Not mine." Then, having satisfied the requirement for "sharing," he turned away, placed his hands in a mudra and closed his eyes, tuning me and the rest of the world out. He never asked me a single question in the sharing sessions and, after two or three attempts to draw him out, I gave up and left him alone.

Reassessment

More than anything else, it was this experience somewhere around 13 years into my spiritual seeking process that forced me to reevaluate my spiritual goals and many of the spiritual philosophies I had so unthinkingly and automatically absorbed—in particular the ideal of detachment.

My seatmate was, indeed, coldly detached, something I once would have admired and aspired to. And yet seeing his example up close, seeing how in the name of spiritual advancement he had cauterized his emotions surrounding his family and anybody else in the world, how he was unengaged and unconcerned with maintaining any sort of social communication, and how (it quickly became obvious) he was also not worried about bathing and personal hygiene, I was left feeling nothing but repulsion and pity.

It was a long retreat. And it gave me more than enough time to reflect upon my love affair with detachment. I remember sneaking peeks at my "partner" one hot afternoon during a long meditation session, watching as sweat soaked through his graying t-shirt, running in rivulets down his none-too-clean, impassive face, hoping the scent of his body odor would waft the other way, thinking, "Is this how I want to be? Is my greatest goal in life to not give a shit about other people and their feelings and their needs and concerns? To not care about the world and what happens to it?"

I decided this was not what I wanted at all.

Along with detachment, I'd also been taught that the true state of existence is inclusive—that "All is One." Moving into a more universal, all-loving, all-inclusive state of consciousness was the hallmark of enlightenment. That week I realized that if that were indeed the case, I was missing the boat in a big way. Far from feeling a connection with all things, I was feeling ever-more isolated and alone. My best times, my happiest times, were all spent with my eyes closed, shut away from the world. Was this really even living?

I realized that, for me, it was not a growth-filled path to divorce myself from the world and from love and involvement. I also couldn't escape seeing how my distancing had made me feel superior (a vibe my seatmate exuded big time) thinking I was successfully being "in the world and not of it." And yet, in truth, all I'd been doing was using spiritual detachment as an excuse to not get hurt, to not feel disappointment, to not become invested in anything that might trigger emotional pain. I determined that, once I got home, I would do my best to understand the entirety of Sri Chinmoy's admonition, not just the section that serviced what obviously had been a pressing need on my part for self-protection.

Leaving the rigorous, highly intellectual and dogmatic spiritual school I'd attended for more than seven years was my first step in liberation. My second step towards greater worldly involvement and availability was leaving the six-year affair with my married lover. Not surprisingly, within a few months I met a lovely man at a local meditation group, a chiropractor who would eventually become my second husband. The third thing I did was follow up on a long-ignored dream to become a psychologist, enrolling in a master's degree program in counseling at a local college. Two years after that break-through retreat I could barely recognize myself. I was married, working in my husband's medical office, approaching graduation, pregnant, enormously involved in life and other people's lives and happier than I'd ever been before.

Real freedom

It would be nice to end my personal story on such a "happy ever after" note. To write that from that moment on I was engaged and fulfilled and rarely suffered. And yet nothing could be further from the truth. The pregnancy ended in a miscarriage and the marriage itself ended in divorce several years after that. And all of it was painful. And yet the depth of the pain and suffering expanded me. It grew me into a better and more compassionate person, a person who could relate to others who were also suffering, a person who cared even more for the condition of others and helping them heal—not in an entangled, drama-filled way, but in a cleanly understanding way.

Since then, I've realized that if I'm not involved and inclusive in life there is no experience and thus no growth. Is there a price to pay for involvement? Absolutely. Is it worth it? Absolutely. The ancient days of the hermit ascetics living in dirty loin cloths up in the Himalayas are a thing of the past—or at least a somewhat dated if not completely inappropriate approach to spirituality for most Westerners. Now, more than ever before, if positive global transformation is to occur, the world needs passionate involvement and profound conscious engagement. And yet I can't count the number of "spiritual" women and men I meet who lament at how difficult life is and how much they want to retreat from the world for good.

"Beam me up, Scotty!" they cry as they avoid politics and television, the news and controversy and confrontation, refusing to take a position, refusing to stand up for something because they don't want to get their energies "entrapped." And yet, dare I say it? Why else are we here if not to be fully involved in life?

The problem isn't the world. The problem is we haven't learned how to live in the world inclusively. It is our very avoidance and judgment that cripples us—our very lack of involvement and refusal to embrace ALL life that makes us suffer. Being involved with everything in a non-judgmental and non-discriminatory way can bring great joy. Being selectively involved—judging some things right and "good" and other things as bad and "wrong," choosing some things and some people over others and then hugely identifying with a "side" on a personal emotional level—that's the formula for creating drama and entanglement.

But we don't have to get into drama. We can choose a side we feel aligned with and invest our time and energies supporting people and issues that we deem important. For example, I've gotten deeply involved in the medical marijuana movement. But I consciously work at not being attached to what happens. I hope more states legalize marijuana. I work towards greater medical recognition, more clinical studies and increased applications, but I'm not emotionally invested in the results of my involvement.

Is that easy to do? Hardly. Is it worthwhile making the effort to stay involved, doing what I can to work for positive change while staying free of emotional identification and entanglement? Yes. Very much so.

We think detachment is the key to freedom because we've all read books and heard lectures that say it is. But then we confuse detachment with avoidance, not realizing that staying remote and uninvolved is death—a slower, numb version of suffering that doesn't benefit anyone. It's taken over 30 years, but I'm slowly marrying both sides of Chinmoy's advice.

I'm more and more in love with the world. Sometimes I'm not in love with certain aspects of it. Frankly the consequences the world is facing because of deeply entrenched conservatism in governments globally—especially conservative interests in the US—are devastating. It's hard to love legislators doing their best to promote personal and corporate self-interests over the health of people and the planet. But the more I get *involved*, doing what I can to raise my own consciousness and the consciousness of humanity, the more fiercely I appreciate life itself.

And so here's the kicker: The more I appreciate life itself, the more determined I become to stay in love with *all* life rather than pieces of it. And the more I do *that*, the greater sea of love my heart becomes.

Detachment, I have discovered, naturally follows wholeness. And freedom comes with it.

Katherine Ellis is a retired psychologist living in Phoenix, Arizona. She is happily married (three times is a charm!), has three grown up step-children, two grandchildren, a cat and two dogs. She still does yoga and meditates daily.

Chapter 7

I was always told that I had to think positive thoughts. The flip side of that was that I came to believe (like a lot of other people) that it was detrimental to my health and wellbeing to think about or acknowledge negative things. This focus on always being upbeat and positive came to a head around 2006 when the film *The Secret* came out. Suddenly it seemed no one could express sadness or frustration without being told to think positive, put on a fake smile and keep on trucking. And yet shoving negative emotions away like they don't exist is toxic. It's like cleaning up by stuffing all your junk in closets and drawers so they're overflowing, so the room looks clean. But if you open anything, all that crap spills out everywhere and there's nowhere to store anything new or good.

Marie Benard

The Pitfalls Of Positive Thinking

Positive thinking has been a big part of the New Age movement. Having a positive mental attitude has been encouraged by New Thought leaders, gurus, and even late-night infomercial hosts. It's a great way to sell books and DVDs. But does it really work?

No doubt just like you, I've heard people tell me to "Turn that frown upside down" and to "Look on the bright side" more times than I can remember. But back in 2005, I was in a dark hole of depression. Thinking of the glass as "half full" was really difficult. Depression has a funny way of making it really hard to see the good in anything.

A little summary about why I was so depressed. I have a major history of trauma and abandonment that left me highly vulnerable and lacking in the skills needed to thrive. My mom had schizoaffective disorder (basically a combination of schizophrenia and bipolar disorder). Before the age of two, she kidnapped me and ran across the country. She thought she was protecting me from my father. I never saw him again. And I'll never really know if this was based on reality or delusion.

Unfortunately, my mother wasn't able to be a full-time single parent and manage her mental health at the same time. By the age of four, I was in and out of foster care. At age seven, I became a permanent ward of the foster care system until I moved out on my own at age fifteen.

Foster care was brutal. There was a lot of abuse and neglect. But it's hard to say if life would have been any better with my mother. For the first few decades of my life, I spent a lot of time in social isolation. From early childhood until my early 30's, I experienced toxic and abusive relationships and went through a series of major depressive episodes. Emotional vulnerability left me physically and mentally vulnerable to predatory people.

Life itself felt pointless—a constant, painful struggle. There were times when I would pray for the energy to get up and end my life. I gained and lost 50-80 pounds a few times. (Over-eating was the healthiest coping strategy I had at the time.) The fog would eventually lift and I'd start to piece my life back together. Then depression or a personal crisis would arise and it would fall apart again. And the cycle continued.

One higher point in the cycle was around age 23 when I got a summer job as a singer at a local tourist attraction—the Capilano Suspension Bridge in British Columbia, Canada—which was amazing and so good for my soul! After that ended, I decided to jump into broadcasting school, which had been on my mind since my early teens. Within a couple weeks of applying for student loans and making a huge deposit at the school, my mom suffered a series of strokes that landed her on her death bed. She remained in hospital, unable to speak, until she passed away several months later, about halfway through the broadcasting program.

During this personal crisis, I had some casual friends, but nobody I truly felt close to or safe with. Loneliness, poor boundaries, and lack of life skills continued to lead me into unhealthy relationships that did more harm than good. Even though I was living off student loans and credit cards, broadcasting school was a blessing. The creative comedy-and-music-filled environment provided enough structure and self-expression to cope with the loss of my mom. I was able to finish the program and even lost 80 pounds that year. About that time I also was helped to find counseling.

The game of positivity

I was in my mid-twenties when I discovered the movie *What the Bleep Do We Know* at the local video store and it seemed like the answer to all my problems. After that came *The Secret*, and I was hooked on the idea that if I could just get my mood high enough and focus on nice-feeling thoughts, I'd attract wealth and happiness into my life. Maybe all my problems could be solved! In retrospect, what a great way to sell me a whole bunch of books! Tell me all my problems will be solved without any work. Just ignore the hurt eating away at my soul and force myself to be believe that everything will be okay! Hooray!

In 2007, a kind occupational therapist helped me build up the courage to work towards my long-time goal of having my own radio talk show. The show, "Synchronicity," launched in July, 2008. Each week, I got to interview a new author. It started out as a spirituality-based show, with guests like Neale Donald Walsh, Eckhart Tolle, SARK, and even a few teachers from *What the Bleep* and *The Secret*. As my spiritual journey evolved, so did the show.

Through the show and my search to "fix" myself, I learned about angels, getting into the flow-state, and started listening to programs from people who said they were channelling information from higher-consciousness beings. I started calling on my angels for good parking spots and called them "parking angels." Most of the time, it worked pretty well. I still call on the parking angels once in a while for fun. Do parking angels really exist? Who the hell knows? It's a harmless superstition that sometimes gives my brain a hit of dopamine when I get what I want. Success! The universe is on my side today!

What wasn't so harmless is how I started to believe (or at least hope) that I could just think and feel my way toward a better life without having the skills or ability to do the physical work of building a life worth living. I don't want to totally slam this idea of positive thinking. Everyone can benefit from a healthy dose of optimism. The operative word being *healthy.*

But the thing is, I wasn't healthy when this slew of positive affirmation information came my way. I was clinically depressed and in a life-long cycle of trauma and self-neglect. I was in physical, mental, and emotional pain. I didn't have the skills to cope with the normal ups and downs of life. I certainly didn't have the skills to consistently keep my thoughts, energy, and vibration in check. Unfortunately, like a lot of people, I thought if I could just force myself to feel better, life would be easy and then I'd be happy. I was desperately searching for the thing that would *fix* me and my life. Also, I thought if I couldn't stay happy and if I couldn't force and control life to go the way I wanted, then it must somehow be my fault.

I even heard one motivational speaker tell a story about how a couple he knew decided to start experiencing a luxurious lifestyle in order to attract it. This married couple racked up their credit cards achieving these better feelings of ease and abundance, *and then they won the lottery.* BINGO! This was the answer to my problems!

I was already pretty familiar with living off credit, so this wasn't a big stretch for me. But at that time I had a day job answering phones for an adult entertainment company. Most of the time the job was fairly manageable. But that industry attracts a lot of wounded souls, and I was exposed to a lot of creepiness and negativity. I had a front-row seat to the underbelly of people's most base desires just when I wanted to surround myself with positivity all the time! So I did what I thought I was being told to do by all the spiritual teachers. I avoided and ignored the things that frustrated me or felt scary or negative. I held onto positive thinking like a life raft and quit the job with nothing lined up. I didn't want to be irresponsible, so it's not like I went hog-wild with spending. But living off credit and savings isn't sustainable no matter how many lottery tickets you buy.

One "positive-thinking" couple I knew invested in extremely high-priced coaching. They upgraded their whole life with holidays and a nicer house they didn't have the money to pay for. Unfortunately, they didn't have the emotional and psychological skills to level-up that quickly. First, they lost their home. Then it wasn't long before their marriage fell apart.

Some other people I knew thought they could play the game of Positivity Will Let Me Cash In on the Stock Market. The odds of winning are better than the lottery and it's more professional. But a few years ago, a good friend of mine doing this lost everything—including his life. I didn't know the market had taken a nose dive that week, so when I asked how his stocks were doing, I believed him when he said it was all good. (What else can a positive thinker say?) The last time I saw him, I was heading to a shift at my volunteer job as a suicide prevention hotline counselor. He asked me about the people who called, and how sure they were about suicide? We had an interesting discussion about my work. Of course, if I'd known his stocks had tanked, I would have questioned how he was managing the feelings of loss. But I had no idea. Two days later, he killed himself.

He hid his emotions very well. I know it's not my fault that he died. The context of our conversation didn't trigger me to ask if he was suicidal. But I still wish I'd asked. Now, regardless of the context, if the topic of suicide comes up, I ask. But what an extreme case of positive thinking gone awry! He viewed himself as a savvy investor and had brokered some trades for friends and colleagues. I guess the shame he felt over losing their money and his identity as a winner was more than he could take.

Out of the trap

You might ask, "So, am I not supposed to have hopes and dreams and think positively?" Of course you are. But when we place all our hopes, dreams, energy, and focus into one outcome it sets us up for massive pain and a setback in our mental and emotional wellbeing. This is something my psychologist calls "hope poisoning." Basically, this means the more we hope and wish for things to be different than they are, the less satisfied we become with our present circumstances. The bigger the contrast of the dream from the current reality of our life, the more unnecessary pain we cause ourselves. Hope and striving can become an addiction. We keep hoping the next thing will fill up our soul. But it never does. Even when we get what we think we want, it only feels great for a short time. It doesn't fulfill us.

Positive thinking isn't good or bad. Like anything, it's neutral, and its value is what we assign to it. What can make it more or less effective is how we go about it. If we're wishing and thinking about things in our future that we want to have, that could be a nice mental vacation. But hope poisoning is a risk if we have a desperate *need* for our fantasies to play out the way we want them to. A more effective way to think positively is to have gratitude for the things that we already have and to focus on the pleasant sensations in this moment. We have to stop thinking in black-or-white, all-or-nothing terms.

There's no harm spending five minutes every so often imagining what you'd do if you had a bottomless bank account. Holding the thought lightly and playing with it while at the same time appreciating and being grateful for what you do have allows it to expand. But focusing on a new life situation while resenting and feeling miserable over current conditions keeps us in the misery box. It can also paralyze us from doing the physical and psychological work necessary to achieve our goals.

So what was it that helped me get out of this hope poisoning trap? A combination of Dialectical Behavior Therapy (DBT), Wellness Recovery Action Plan (WRAP), self-compassion, and gratitude. DBT is an evidence-based and mindfulness-based therapy developed by psychologist Marsha Linehan which teaches skills on Distress Tolerance, Emotion Regulation, and Interpersonal Effectiveness, interwoven through a foundation of mindfulness.

WRAP is an evidence-based wellness and prevention process that anyone can use to manage their physical and mental health. It's based on the key concepts of hope, personal responsibility, education, self-advocacy, and support. Note that "responsibility" isn't the same as blame or fault. It's my *responsibility* to do what I can to stay as well as I can and keep moving forward, no matter what life throws at me. It's not my *fault* if unpleasant things happen, or if negative thoughts and emotions arise.

Mindfulness is a pretty big buzz word these days, but it basically means being aware and accepting of the current, momentary reality. We don't have to *like* the reality, but we can accept it rather than getting sucked into our thoughts, judgements, plans, worries, and the barrage of other crap that runs through our minds. There are so many ways to practice mindfulness, but in DBT, mindfulness is broken into "what" we're doing and "how" we're doing it. DBT teaches numerous practices that help develop the ability to walk the middle path between logic and emotion, which they call "wise mind."

With mindfulness, we can start to develop our discernment for choosing the most effective approach, depending on the situation. It's been a long road and I don't always get it right. I still have hard days, and even challenging months or seasons. Even writing this chapter has brought up all those old fears about not being good enough or not having enough experience. Why would anyone listen to what works for me? I'm not famous or a billionaire. After years of DBT practice, however, I can recognize that those are just thoughts. Just because I think them doesn't make them true! And even if they are true, how do we ever get any better without doing stuff that makes us feel a little scared sometimes?

I still have fears, and problems, and insecurities. I'm still highly sensitive and susceptible to depression and negative thoughts. But I'm no longer a *victim* of my thoughts and emotions. After consistent practice, my whole life has changed for the better. If depression or a crisis come, my life no longer falls apart. I've been able to take the painful first few decades and transform them into something useful to others. I'm now working as a Peer Support Worker on a highly intensive, stressful psychiatric unit. I'm coping with the stress in healthy ways while making a difference in the lives of others. I've also been blessed to have the opportunity to become a facilitator in the Wellness Recovery Action Plan (WRAP), which is incredibly rewarding. I've even started performing stand-up comedy—not because I want to be a performer, but because my body trembles at the very *thought* of it. I spent decades avoiding pain and scary stuff. Now, I focus on using challenging experiences as an opportunity to build my life skills.

That's a massive change for the better. And this is the work that is allowing me to experience real happiness in my own life and to feel more connected to the world around me. And if I can do it, anyone can do it. It's exactly *because* I'm not perfect or famous or powerful that this message is so important.

Not everyone is dealt the same hand in life. Some people *do* have it easier than others. But *everyone* can do *something* to grow a little more each day. Even if that "something" is just being a little kinder to yourself. That alone can make your life, and the rest of the world, a little brighter.

Marie Benard is the host of Synchronicity: Talk Radio for Your Mind, Body, and Soul. Through her radio show and YouTube channel, Marie's interviews and vlogs have touched the lives of millions of listeners and viewers. Marie also serves as a wellness recovery workshop facilitator and a mental health support worker. Her wellness journey was necessitated by a challenging upbringing that left her isolated, vulnerable to abuse, and lacking the basic life skills necessary to transition into adulthood. The radio show was an integral part of her recovery journey. Marie eventually discovered the mindfulness-based, Dialectical Behavior Therapy. Through the support of a good therapist, loving friends, and the wealth of information she gleaned through years as a radio interviewer, Marie slowly began to build a life worth living. She now is blessed to have the opportunity to give back to the community and help others who have struggled with trauma, mental health challenges, and a lack of purpose. Marie can be found practicing being in the present moment by performing improv comedy, singing karaoke, playing board games with friends, enjoying a walk on the beautiful Vancouver seawall, or through her website www.MarieBenard.com

Chapter 8

All the world religions basically agree that enlightenment is the purpose of life. It may be called different things: enlightenment, nirvana, awakening, paradise, self-realization, but essentially it means the same thing be it Hindu, Christian, Buddhist, Muslim, etc. I made my life's goal to become enlightened because I was always drawn to the transcendent and believed it was possible. The New Age hype around enlightenment—the "We gotta get out of this place" focus—only heightened my resolve. The pursuit was beyond humbling. And it revealed a lot of misunderstandings that exist about what enlightenment and ascension even are. It also taught me that innocent devotion without direction or a deeper understanding can be a dangerous undertaking.

Louise SaintOnge

In Pursuit Of Something More

I'm not enlightened. I haven't ascended. I'm not awakened. And I don't have any answers for you. What I do have is a story about me, a life-long lover of the divine who couldn't quite figure out how to live a 'normal' life and gave everything I had to become enlightened, to be fully awakened. And damn it, I'm still here and none of those things have happened! Now what? My passion for enlightenment took me from the exquisite transcendent to rock bottom existential meaninglessness.

When I was a little girl I loved the images on holy cards. I wanted to be like the Virgin Mary, or one of the saints with halos, or maybe a nun wearing those giant wooden rosary beads who had a special connection to God. I always asked the big questions. Who am I? Why am I here? I looked at things with such curiosity and didn't understand why the world so often showed up different than the way I was thinking it was supposed to be. It seemed so opposite, upside down, scary, unsafe, difficult. *This can't be all there is. There's got to be more.*

In the 60s and 70s, exploring consciousness and mind expansion were shaking up everything and everyone, and when the spiritual teachings from the East came floating into my awareness, they ignited the spiritual embers smoldering deep within me, fueling my passion to learn more. I was in constant pursuit of personal development and devoured everything on psychology, philosophy, spirituality, alternative medicine, and quantum physics. I was transported by the stories of saints and sages and I, too, wanted to transcend the human condition and end the cycle of birth and death as they did.

Trying to fit all that into figuring out what I wanted to 'be' in life, what career I should pursue, was daunting. Nothing really stood out for me on those long checklists of occupations. *What's wrong with me that none of them interest me?* I could have been a nun if I were Catholic or Buddhist, or some other organized religion. That's how devoted I felt. But every religion seemed narrow minded and too proscriptive to me. I loved having fun, singing, dancing, and being a little crazy, and I probably couldn't do that if I were a nun!

The enormous challenge I faced was "How do I live that passion in this 'normal' life? How do I reconcile what seems like opposite worlds of heaven and earth? What were the holy people talking about? How do I live a rich, meaningful, divinely-inspired life in our modern day?" On more than a few occasions I'd be prostrate on the floor in tears praying, "Let me give my life for truth and understanding. I offer my life to know the divine! Show me how." This is what I wanted more than anything, and I hid it from most everyone.

Living in the world

I didn't know how to be happy at my jobs and make a steady living. I had my share of success as a director of this and that, as a university dean, a Montessori teacher, a university professor. The list goes on. I was always fast tracked into leadership positions, but all were short-lived and I would quickly become disillusioned. I couldn't figure out how to play the game of office politics nor could I understand how people could be so manipulative and self-serving. Sometimes I felt so innocent and naïve. *Why can't I play those games? What's wrong with me?*

Just get over yourself, Louise! You have to be happy in whatever situation you are in.

This was the spiritual philosophy I constantly beat myself up with and was always coming up short. I felt out of place and discouraged.

On more than one occasion I would be in my car in the parking lot at work in tears, dreading going in to face the day.

Try as I may, the external world held little interest for me. I continued with my commitment to awakening on every level. I practiced many forms of meditation, was initiated into deep shamanic and esoteric earth-based traditions, and received training in many energy healing methods. After one initiation I fell to the floor and began simultaneously laughing and crying as every thought disappeared from my mind. I lay there searching in every corner, and everywhere I searched, my mind was completely empty—the vast expanse of emptiness was profound and utterly liberating. Within twenty-four hours random thoughts slowly crept back in and there "I" was again.

Decades passed. And then, in meditation one day, I saw myself in the Himalayas in India. I was struck by the vision's vividness but was even more blown away when I very clearly heard a voice that said, "Welcome home my beloved daughter." I was completely taken by surprise. I had never heard a voice in meditation before. There was such a profound familiarity to it I began to sob, the tears pouring down my face, unstoppable. At that moment I knew I had to follow this voice. I had to go to India. If I didn't, I knew the path I was on would surely lead to an early death.

There was a brief moment when I wondered how can I do this? How do I leave my job? My son who was just 16? (I was a single mom.) My house? My stuff? But the pull was so strong that it no longer felt like a choice. I had no idea what would happen once I got there. All I knew was if I was going to be happy, feel fulfilled, connected, and truly purposeful, I had to follow this voice without question. It was full-on heartfelt devotion, surrender and trust. My prayers felt answered and I saw this as my ticket to liberation, finally! I loved my son and my heart ached to leave him, but I also trusted him and his wisdom and knew if

I didn't follow this he wouldn't even have a mom. Or, perhaps even worse, he'd have a mom that settled for convention and didn't follow her deepest calling. And what kind of wretched example would I be for him then?

I got rid of everything I owned except for two suitcases—no storage units, no friend's basements to keep my things in. I wasn't planning on returning. Some people thought I was crazy, some people were jealous and wished they had the courage to do such a dramatic thing, some judged me harshly as selfish and irresponsible. A few cheered me on as I pulled the plug on my reality as I knew it and allowed everything to crumble and fall away.

Wandering sadhu

In India, attaining enlightenment, or *moksha*, is at the core of everything, so whether you walk around naked, covered in ash, or sit on the side of the road in meditation, no one questions it. It's part of life. I finally felt free to express my devotion outwardly. For the first year I wandered like a modern-day sadhu (a holy person who gives up material life), traveling with another woman who shared the same passion and goal of ascension, following an inner compass, visiting holy sites, traveling where foreigners had rarely or never been.

I meditated sitting. I meditated walking. I visualized. I chanted. I gave. I forgave. I had my mind and heart blown open from experiences with people and places that shattered so many beliefs and assumptions I had about life, about good and bad, right and wrong. I trusted. I prayed. I laughed. I cried. I wrote songs. I sang in the forest. And I waited. Waited for the eternal transcendent moment when I would pierce through all the veils and permanently understand and experience absolute Truth and the nature of reality. Waited, for some ascended master to recognize my devotion and my efforts and bestow grace and enlightenment upon me.

I knew it was just a matter of time.

While staying in Rewalsar, a magical and holy village in Himachal Pradesh in northern India, my traveling companion told me that she felt her "time" of ascension was coming very close. She said she could feel it and chose to stay in her room until the moment occurred. She gave away most of her remaining belongings and had the guesthouse manager bring her food now and then. I had a sort of panic. "What? She's ready to ascend?" Jealousy rose within me.

How could she do that before me? What is she doing that I haven't done?

Maybe I hadn't meditated enough or visualized enough, or prayed enough? Maybe my mind wasn't clear enough? Maybe she was kinder or more generous to people? *Crap!* Whatever the reasons, I had to ramp up my efforts. But then I wondered, *What does ascension look like?* Will she disappear? Will her body still be there leaving me to deal with disposing of it somehow? What will I tell her family? I had never really thought about the practical side of ascension. (When I read this I think, "Wow, we must have been crazy.")

Well, she didn't ascend, and I was relieved. So onward I went.

Descent

Throughout this wild journey I experienced long stretches of seeing the divine perfection of all things—the suffering, the filth the wealth, and the beauty. I had no questions, no needs, no aspirations and seemed to be flowing in a stream of such blissful contentment and unbroken happiness I felt my heart could explode with the exquisite dance of it all.

Then I hit a wall.

I was exhausted from traveling, wracked with a serious bout of dysentery, and beginning to question *everything*. I needed a retreat, somewhere I could go and just stop for a few days. I registered for a 10-day silent mediation retreat at a Goenka Vipassana Meditation Center. It was February, bitter cold, no heating, no hot water in the bathrooms, a freezing meditation hall, everyone wrapped in multiple wool blankets, women on the right, men on the left. Echoing through the cavernous, nearly empty hall were the sounds of Indians burping, sneezing, clearing their throats with no attempt to muffle the sound. *What the hell am I doing here?* Wait! Stop! I just have to be more mindful, more quiet in my mind. This is for me to get over. They don't seem to have a problem with this.

My thoughts raged on.

What happened to the bliss? *I can't do this!* Squash all desires. Attain desirelessness. Just observe sensations and cravings. *OMG I have to get to the bathroom, quick!* Worst diarrhea I can remember. Quietly creeping back to sit on the freezing floor, screaming pain in my left leg and hip. I've got to adjust my position. But I'm not supposed to move!

After the first 10-day session I was a mess. No way I could go back out into the world. I was falling apart. Why did some people seem uplifted and happy? No cravings. *What does that mean?* Desirelessness. *What does that mean?* Even my passion for enlightenment was a desire! And what about things that make me happy? Is that false? Is that a craving? Am I supposed to eliminate anything that brings joy?

I did another 10-day session.

I was outside doing my evening walking meditation, questioning every thought I had, freezing in the biting cold of the Himalayas, worried that any thought I had could be a desire or craving. I looked up and saw the brilliant stars splashed across the night sky and began to cry. Was seeing this beauty and loving it so much a craving? *Do I have to let this go too? Where then is the joy? What's the point of life?*

By the end of my second retreat I was even more distraught. My meditations had tapped into a vein of universal suffering that was almost unbearable and I sat on my bed sobbing. I can't go out into the world even yet!

After the 3rd 10-day retreat I gained some measure of calm and left the retreat center. Eventually I settled in a flat in Bhagsu, a village near McLeod Ganj where the Dalai Lama has residence. I was grateful to finally stop wandering and have a home where I could recover some semblance of myself as I knew it. I tried to lighten up and turned my focus outwardly. I befriended street people and shared meals with their families. I visited hospitals and sang songs to sick children. But everything began to take on a shoddy veneer quality that I could see through. There was no more depth, no more color, no more beauty, no point!

What has happened?

Once upon a time I saw everything as sacred and holy. I would have tears in my eyes when I heard the song of a bird, or saw the stars sparkling in the night sky. I would be lifted to great heights when I chanted a mantra or listened to sacred music. All this was gone. I cry even now as I recall that ashen moment when I felt I had lost all communion with life and instead began to see everything as just a concept, an illusion of the mind, a point of view, just like the holy books say.

Instead of self-realization I saw through everything and I didn't like what I saw. It all seemed false and inauthentic. I was completely disillusioned (Great word-without illusion!) and angry. To hell with spirituality! To hell with God. To hell with prayer and meditation, ascended masters and holy sages. Screw enlightenment. Fuck doing anything!

There's no point to any of it!

Four years in India and I was undone, disappearing, and there was no ship in sight. No sign of land. I plodded through my days like a zombie. The world was dead to me and I was dead to the world. I didn't have a teacher to guide me. I didn't have a road map of how to do this. Bad idea! I recently heard Sadhguru, an Indian mystic and teacher in Tamil Nadu, say that dismantling your psychological structure (your trap) dismantles your security, your purpose, and that if you dismantle without first achieving balance you will go crazy.

Wish I had known that then.

Back into the light

It would be great to tell you that I finally broke through and became self-realized. But I cannot. My quest had taken a serious toll on my health and I returned to America exhausted and depleted. It took me three more agonizing years to crawl out of the dark abyss of non-existence and meaninglessness.

So, what now?

I'm still here, a story in motion with more chapters to experience. Color has returned. Once again I am awed by the beauty of nature, the song of a bird, and am transported by the sound of sacred music.

I am no longer interested in pursuing enlightenment. If it happens it's going to happen, regardless of how hard I try, or how much I want it, whatever "it" is. I'm done with all the efforting. The gravitational pull towards the transcendent is ever present, but I have learned how to tether myself to earth. I realize I, as human, am a bridge between heaven and earth and being here in this world, in this body now, is my daily practice.

I am no longer in passionate pursuit to do or be anything in particular. I am open to life's sweetness. I find freedom and strength resting in the simple, yet profound truth of who I truly am, a pure, unfettered, presence from which all things arise. I am dancing and singing and at times laugh hysterically at all of it.

As I re-read this story I can easily say to myself, "WTF was I thinking?" But when you have a calling, a deep urging that comes from within and continues to override everything, what do you do? Most deny it, play it safe, and try to fit in as best as possible, living in a way that avoids being judged or ostracized, a way that avoids straining the fabric of their reality. We end up hiding who we really are, what we most love, and miss out on experiencing what we alone are uniquely designed to express.

I wouldn't change a thing.

So, what is it that brings you to your knees? What have you kept deeply hidden inside of you that keeps calling you, however crazy it may sound, however much you fear being judged?

Follow it! It is the bud of a beautiful flower waiting to blossom— a flower that won't look anything like you imagined it would at the start of your journey. And what if that's the whole point?

Louise SaintOnge - My chapter is my real bio. I've been a life-long student of consciousness, yet kept this rather hidden for most of my life behind the veil of cultural and social "shoulds" – master's degree, professional positions, and the like. The duplicity of it nearly killed me. Fast forward to now without the veil. I am a highly sensitive empath, energy healer, spiritual counselor, ceremonial artist, medium, and a lover of nature. My clients say I embody an unusual "wise woman" energy, reflecting a life of deep exploration and experience that empowers them to trust their inner knowing and acknowledge their own gifts. I support people to become powerfully grounded, vibrantly healthy, and exquisitely aligned with what is deep and true for *them*. I believe my work is unique. By blending my intuitive gifts with energy

81

work, clients can move through stuck places more quickly, discover their path and their potential, and be inspired with the confidence and courage to make the changes necessary to live their dreams. I am also an energy healer of people, animals and places. As a Medium I connect people with family and friends who have passed, providing healing and profound moments of loving connection. Come and visit me and I'll tell you more! **www.louisesaintonge.com**

Chapter 9

"Thinking makes it so" sounds so simple and straightforward. It suggests one new thought will allow me to pull the strings of the universe, lining me up to receive all my personal desires and wishes. Unfortunately, it's not that easy. Manifestation involves a lot more than making an affirmation and posting it on the refrigerator door. And yet most people I know in the spiritual community have ended up falling prey to believing exactly that. This is magical thinking. And it's something we all need to watch out for on the path to becoming greater.

PATRICK CAMERON

BEYOND MAGICAL THINKING

Attending a workshop a number of years ago our facilitator asked those of us in attendance to write down the most difficult or challenging situation that was most prevalent in our lives at the moment. Then we were asked to crumble up the piece of paper that held our challenge and throw it to the front of the room. Then our facilitator discussed how all of us are meaning-making machines, that our personal experiences create our perceptions. (Perceptions are defined as the ability to see, hear, or become aware of something through the senses.) Then she talked about our tendency to view our current life challenge as highly difficult simply because it was ours.

We create our story from our perceptions and, as she wisely counselled that day, "All perceptions are misperceptions" because they are subjective, reflecting our own meaning-making ability. After she had shared her insight on our need for story making and how we personalize our stories, she invited us to go to the front of the room and choose a crumpled up piece of paper from the many scattered around the room and take it on as our own. Did it seem difficult?

Her point was well made.

Personal meaning making and perception are the ground from which all of our thinking arises, and some of this thinking can be magical in that magical thinking allows us to reach a conclusion without any evidence to support that conclusion. As our facilitator's exercise illustrated, it's very easy to feel our problems and difficulties are worse than any one else's. Everyone's life is better than mine, and my problem or situation is worse than any other. And we reach that conclusion based on very little information indeed.

Illusionary links

Magical thinking as it is used in anthropology, philosophy, and psychology, suggests that something will happen as a result of simply thinking in a certain way, embodying a certain belief deeply enough or wishing something strongly enough, without any effort, action or interaction with an intended outcome. Magical thinking could be believing in things *more strongly* than either evidence or experience justifies. Magical thinking is an expression of our capacity to participate in an inflated sense of power and influence over other people's lives, conditions and influencing outcomes.

In psychiatry magical thinking is a disorder of thought content. It denotes the false belief that one's thoughts, actions, or words will cause or prevent a specific consequence in some way that defies commonly understood laws of causality. For example, "My competitor's business went bankrupt as a result of my intention of some misfortune arising." It goes back as far as the advent of human superstition. "Let's throw the young virgin into the volcano to assure a successful harvest." Or "I will become enlightened by imagining images of light and ignoring the darkness."

When my daughter Megan was around age five she created a magical thinking ritual. When riding in the car and encountering a red light she would make her declaration. "This is magic Megan speaking, red light I command you to turn green NOW!" Occasionally she would time her declaration at the perfect moment that the signal would actually change from red to green. She would then squeal with glee feeling all powerful and mighty since she had prevented us from having to slow down or stop on our way to our destination. My wife and I found this entertaining and amusing even though, as we all know, eventually all red lights turn green.

Megan's red light ritual reflects the naivety and fresh innocence of many who first come to metaphysics and spiritual practices, delighting in the idea that their thoughts affect reality in a magical way. Magical thinking is a phase we all travel through when we are first introduced to the idea that we can influence our lives through shifting our attitudes, habits, beliefs. and consciousness. Magical thinking is actually a reasonable and understandable stage and state of the evolutionary journey that we all encounter. Unfortunately, many seekers continue to use spiritual practice from the perspective of acquiring things or controlling life versus contributing something. Many spiritual seekers never evolve out of the acquisition stage.

It is important to have magic in our lives, to be delighted by life's surprises and unexpected good fortune. We can all use more magic in our lives. However, the kind of magical thinking expressed in Megan's red light ritual, viewing God or Source as separate from ourselves and the equivalent of a spiritual vending machine designed to deliver our every desire, is a perspective that we must grow beyond. For example, how many times have you heard or possibly said yourself, "Please God help me in winning the lottery!" This is a frequent request I have encountered over the years. Many people really think asking (or even commanding) God/Source to deliver houses, cars, winning lottery tickets and the ideal mate is how abundance works—which is nothing but magical thinking.

Abundance is not about winning the lottery but rather cultivating an awareness that our natural and inherent state of being *is* abundance. However, my experience with many students of metaphysics over the past 25 years has made me aware that most seekers desire to be soothed rather than empowered and desire comfort over transformation. This, quite frankly, is using spiritual practice as a form of spiritual by-pass— as way for the ego to avoid discomfort or disappointment. Demonstrating or manifesting parking spots, prince's and palaces is not what the Buddha had in mind when he said that your thinking creates your life or when Jesus of Nazareth said, "It is done unto you as you believe."

The spiritual ego

The spiritualized ego is a common trait when dealing with magical thinking. It is characterized by the dynamic trio of Me, Myself and I. A spiritualized ego will use any sign of progress to compare itself with others or to create a perception of superiority or dominance. This is the merit badge metaphysician who says, "I read the book, took the workshop, got my certificate and bought the tee shirt. I *got* it." The effort and accomplishment is associated with feelings of being special or in control. A spiritualized ego will keep a person on the surface level of awareness and expectation seeking immediate gratification with a minimum of investment.

Consciousness always precedes experience, and if our consciousness is shallow and self centered our life will reflect those same qualities. The challenge with a spiritualized ego is, it will never allow you the spaciousness and present moment wonder to allow anything new to be revealed. It is too busy being in control, trying to look good. Unfortunately, control is important when driving a car or operating heavy equipment, but not much help in matters of healing, shifting or transforming life.

We took human form in this realm and dimension not to magically say "Abracadabra!" over and over again and POOF! manifest our every desire, but to pursue our passions and longings and in the process of these pursuits develop and grow new capacities to fulfill our souls' longing and hearts' desires. Living our best life from our best self is rare and unique but available to us all. But like any proficiency it requires practice, commitment and resilience. Without developing stronger spiritual muscles, our affirmations are nothing more than

y using our past experiences to help craft and create what our y be. The beauty of magical thinking is that it is a beautiful of Infinite Intelligence seeking and nudging us to become a oorway of possibility, healing, joy and abundance. It can assist ating our blueprint of possibility. Like any great structure, or art it requires our effort, commitment, and follow through. r thoughts create reality. Not magically, but inevitably. What k, we become. And that's magic enough.

k Cameron - Magical thinking launched him into pursuing his of being a successful actor and moving to Los Angeles in 1979, he performed in a number of Hollywood hits and television "My dream prepared me for my calling," he says. The unintended discovered in his acting pursuit involved becoming a master enter, cabinet maker, and general building contractor. For the past years he has devoted himself to practicing, studying, teaching, ting, and lecturing about Spirituality and Consciousness. For the t 17 years he has served as the Spiritual Director of the Edmonton entre for Spiritual Living in Alberta, Canada. His current focus is tegral Spirituality and the various practices and habits that support ving in greater wholeness and possibility. Currently he is engaged with ntegral Coaching Canada programs, coaching individuals and organizations in the building of new capacities and wellness. He has been called a spiritual revolutionary, curious about the ways we can all be more awake to our inherent gifts and talents. A gifted speaker, author, teacher husband, father and grandfather, he can be reached at Integralmastery@gmail.com announcements. Our positive thoughts are hollow, and we can look like delusional lunatics.

Magical thinkers are masters at announcing, "I am wealthy. I am a millionaire. I am powerful. I am famous," thinking that's going to do the deed. And yet declaring an intention is only one step of many steps to a new experience. You must start where you are, work with the skills you have in the moment, and grow the consciousness of increase and supply, gradually, sequentially, and inevitably.

If you are affirming that your income has doubled, perhaps your current developed capacity to fulfill this might simply be to work twice as much. The next step is learning to gradually develop the capacity to work smarter, not harder, and remain open to new possibilities that are in alignment with your stated intention. And yet magical thinking precludes the expenditure of any effort. It is remarkable how many people I have encountered over the years who use the majority of their time, talent, and energy trying to avoid effort and work.

Magical thinkers understand, "Thoughts create reality," but often fail to understand   that the reason they have unwanted repetitive patterns operating in their lives is because they are simply repeating unconscious negative thoughts and feelings. Unfortunately, because magical thinking is a very egoic form of thinking, it becomes very challenging to entertain a new idea or a deeper awareness. A negative magical thinking pattern might sound something like: "I'm afraid my fearful thoughts that it will rain during my outdoor wedding will make it rain." And then, if it does rain on your special day, magical thinking can even run in past tense. "I knew my worries about it raining on my wedding day, would make it rain!" And yet worry and fear have never influenced the weather!

A healthy person, knowing there is a risk of rain at an outdoor summer wedding, embraces the potential, not as a negative but as a

given possibility. And then they plan the wedding guests to bring colourful share on this special day of love "Just in

Thinking versus being

Magical thinking and the spiritualized ego about spiritual topics all the time I am, th Most New Agers I know get caught in this evolving because of all the books they read and they're not *applying the knowledge.* They're practices that assist them in embodying a new w confused thinking *about* something with changir Immersing themselves in spiritual topics, they knowledge is evolving them. They unconsciously l *about* spiritual topics is the same things as manifesti consciousness. But it's just more intellectual informa

A great teacher once said "Realization withou hallucination." A truly enlightened individual will ne enlightened they are because they realize our evolution a for transformation is an ongoing, never-ending journey. presents an opportunity to wake up in a new way. We a time where it is no longer effective to simply know th intellectualize. We must know and then practice and app know.

We don't need to shame ourselves or blame ourselves experiences of unhealthy magical thinking, but rather love our all our imperfection. Magical thinking is only a problem w becomes our primary tool to manage our lives. Waking up do mean we never slip into magical thinking. Waking up means w aware of the moments when we are in a state of magical think Waking up means being awake to our habitual patterns and hab what the Buddha had in mind when he said that your thinking creates your life or when Jesus of Nazareth said, "It is done unto you as you believe."

The spiritual ego

The spiritualized ego is a common trait when dealing with magical thinking. It is characterized by the dynamic trio of Me, Myself and I. A spiritualized ego will use any sign of progress to compare itself with others or to create a perception of superiority or dominance. This is the merit badge metaphysician who says, "I read the book, took the workshop, got my certificate and bought the tee shirt. I *got* it." The effort and accomplishment is associated with feelings of being special or in control. A spiritualized ego will keep a person on the surface level of awareness and expectation seeking immediate gratification with a minimum of investment.

Consciousness always precedes experience, and if our consciousness is shallow and self centered our life will reflect those same qualities. The challenge with a spiritualized ego is, it will never allow you the spaciousness and present moment wonder to allow anything new to be revealed. It is too busy being in control, trying to look good. Unfortunately, control is important when driving a car or operating heavy equipment, but not much help in matters of healing, shifting or transforming life.

We took human form in this realm and dimension not to magically say "Abracadabra!" over and over again and POOF! manifest our every desire, but to pursue our passions and longings and in the process of these pursuits develop and grow new capacities to fulfill our souls' longing and hearts' desires. Living our best life from our best self is rare and unique but available to us all. But like any proficiency it requires practice, commitment and resilience. Without developing stronger spiritual muscles, our affirmations are nothing more than announcements. Our positive thoughts are hollow, and we can look like delusional lunatics.

Magical thinkers are masters at announcing, "I am wealthy. I am a millionaire. I am powerful. I am famous," thinking that's going to do the deed. And yet declaring an intention is only one step of many steps to a new experience. You must start where you are, work with the skills you have in the moment, and grow the consciousness of increase and supply, gradually, sequentially, and inevitably.

If you are affirming that your income has doubled, perhaps your current developed capacity to fulfill this might simply be to work twice as much. The next step is learning to gradually develop the capacity to work smarter, not harder, and remain open to new possibilities that are in alignment with your stated intention. And yet magical thinking precludes the expenditure of any effort. It is remarkable how many people I have encountered over the years who use the majority of their time, talent, and energy trying to avoid effort and work.

Magical thinkers understand, "Thoughts create reality," but often fail to understand that the reason they have unwanted repetitive patterns operating in their lives is because they are simply repeating unconscious negative thoughts and feelings. Unfortunately, because magical thinking is a very egoic form of thinking, it becomes very challenging to entertain a new idea or a deeper awareness. A negative magical thinking pattern might sound something like: "I'm afraid my fearful thoughts that it will rain during my outdoor wedding will make it rain." And then, if it does rain on your special day, magical thinking can even run in past tense. "I knew my worries about it raining on my wedding day, would make it rain!" And yet worry and fear have never influenced the weather!

A healthy person, knowing there is a risk of rain at an outdoor summer wedding, embraces the potential, not as a negative but as a given possibility. And then they plan accordingly. Maybe they invite the wedding guests to bring colourful umbrella's and warm hearts to share on this special day of love "Just in case." And if it rains, it rains!

Thinking versus being

Magical thinking and the spiritualized ego will say, "Because I think about spiritual topics all the time I am, therefore, highly spiritual." Most New Agers I know get caught in this trap. They think they're evolving because of all the books they read and seminars they go to. *But they're not applying the knowledge.* They're not enrolling in new practices that assist them in embodying a new way of being. They have confused thinking *about* something with changing their consciousness. Immersing themselves in spiritual topics, they magically think the knowledge is evolving them. They unconsciously believe that thinking *about* spiritual topics is the same things as manifesting a higher level of consciousness. But it's just more intellectual information.

A great teacher once said "Realization without application is hallucination." A truly enlightened individual will never tell you how enlightened they are because they realize our evolution and opportunity for transformation is an ongoing, never-ending journey. Each new day presents an opportunity to wake up in a new way. We are living in a time where it is no longer effective to simply know things and to intellectualize. We must know and then practice and apply what we know.

We don't need to shame ourselves or blame ourselves for past experiences of unhealthy magical thinking, but rather love ourselves in all our imperfection. Magical thinking is only a problem when it becomes our primary tool to manage our lives. Waking up does not mean we never slip into magical thinking. Waking up means we are aware of the moments when we are in a state of magical thinking. Waking up means being awake to our habitual patterns and habits, consciously using our past experiences to help craft and create what our future may be. The beauty of magical thinking is that it is a beautiful tributary of Infinite Intelligence seeking and nudging us to become a greater doorway of possibility, healing, joy and abundance. It can assist us in creating our blueprint of possibility. Like any great structure, or work of art it requires our effort, commitment, and follow through.

Our thoughts create reality. Not magically, but inevitably. What we think, we become. And that's magic enough.

Patrick Cameron - Magical thinking launched him into pursuing his dream of being a successful actor and moving to Los Angeles in 1979, where he performed in a number of Hollywood hits and television roles. "My dream prepared me for my calling," he says. The unintended gifts discovered in his acting pursuit involved becoming a master carpenter, cabinet maker, and general building contractor. For the past 23 years he has devoted himself to practicing, studying, teaching, writing, and lecturing about Spirituality and Consciousness. For the last 17 years he has served as the Spiritual Director of the Edmonton Centre for Spiritual Living in Alberta, Canada. His current focus is Integral Spirituality and the various practices and habits that support living in greater wholeness and possibility. Currently he is engaged with Integral Coaching Canada programs, coaching individuals and organizations in the building of new capacities and wellness. He has been called a spiritual revolutionary, curious about the ways we can all be more awake to our inherent gifts and talents. A gifted speaker, author, teacher husband, father and grandfather, he can be reached at Integralmastery@gmail.com

Chapter 10

Everything happens for a reason

Believe it or not, Marilyn Monroe is given credit for the origin for this cliché. I chose this topic because in my experience most people need reasons for what happens to them in their lives. And while this is quite normal, it also can be an endless rabbit hole that people dive into that never delivers ultimate truth. It also can be used as an excuse for not taking responsibility because it implies somehow things are out of their control. Clinging to this cliché can also keep many people from looking within themselves to find their own meanings for what has occurred in their lives, choosing for themselves how they want to move forward.

Sharon Ballantine

Everything Happens For A Reason

How does it make you feel when people tell you that "Everything happens for a reason?" You may have just lost your job, your marriage ended or you put a dent in your car. Does it make you feel better to think that everything you go through happens for a reason? What if you can't figure out what the reason is? You may be on a lifetime search looking for reasons for everything!

There was a time in my life where I thought I had good cause to demand reasons from the Universe for what was happening to me. This pivotal time was when I was between ages 21 and 24 years old and lost my core family—my brother, mother, father and grandmother in the course of a three-year period—to different diseases and suicide. I thought knowing the reasons all this happened would make some sort of sense of things and make me feel better. After all, aren't we taught it's important to know the "whys" of things? To grasp the meanings of things in life?

Growing up, I felt we were a pretty normal family. My parents divorced when I was a pre-teen and my brother and I lived with my mom. In our childhood photographs, my brother Ken is bright-eyed and usually smiling or laughing. We were only a year and a half apart and had such fun growing up together. Our parents loved having parties when we were young and we used to marvel at how glamorous everyone looked. Ken and I would pretend like we were going off to bed and spend hours peeking around corners at all the dressed-up guests. We finally got so tired that we almost got caught as we were running and laughing all the way up the stairs to our rooms.

In our teen years, when I had a boyfriend and was socializing with friends at the Bellevue Square Mall, working at Nordstrom and living life, Ken spent the majority of his time at home, even though he had no restrictions put on him by our parents. Freedom just wasn't as important to Ken as it was to me. He seemed content to be at home with his music, at school, or work. But about the time he entered puberty, I noticed a change in him. He was no longer a happy-go-lucky kid. He was a very accomplished young man, an A student, and he also had extraordinary talents. He played several different musical instruments, even though he couldn't read a note of music. I watched him as he listened to songs on the radio or on an album, then picked up one of his instruments, the drums, piano, or guitar, and in a matter of minutes was able to play the song. I was amazed and sat and listened to him for hours.

The change in Ken seemed to be a sullenness that wasn't there in his childhood, a quiet introspection that none of us guessed was depression. He never did drugs or got in any trouble whatsoever. Although he wasn't very social, he had several good friends. As I had done many times over the past several years, I tried to talk to Ken about making the choice to be happy. I told him I felt happiness was a decision, and I gave him examples of how I found joy. He didn't seem to be able to relate to why it made me happy to simply go for a walk, plan the upcoming week-end or rearrange the living room. I didn't understand very much about depression, so I tried to be supportive just by being available to talk when he wanted to.

My dad moved to Chile in South America after my parents divorced when I was 12. After that I only got to see him a couple of times a year. Although dad lived half a world from me, I always felt like we were the same person and very connected. He had a great sense of humor and always made me laugh. We were so alike in personality. Dad was an extrovert that seemed to make friends wherever he went. That trait seemed to come naturally to me too. I also seemed to have inherited my dad's positive outlook on life, particularly when things weren't going great. And I looked just like him. We often seemed to know what the other was thinking. I knew I could always count on my dad to be there for me, and the distance made no difference whatsoever.

After the divorce, Mom worked fulltime and did the best she could to provide for my brother and me while running our household. Mom and I weren't as emotionally close as my dad and I were, much as I wanted us to be. She seemed so often to be in survival mode as she had the responsibility of day-to-day care for us and it felt like she worried about our financial situation. We didn't have many heart-to-heart talks, but I knew my mom loved and supported me. We tried to make an effort to spend time together. But somehow it never really seemed to happen.

Ken and I felt like we should help out, so we eventually got jobs to help with our own expenses. Ken got a paper route at age 12 and my first job (aside from constant babysitting) was at The House of Pies as a hostess at age 16. These jobs helped us pay for our school clothes and any extra activities we wanted. My maternal grandmother lived nearby in the heart of Seattle, Washington, and we saw her pretty often. She came over to our house in Bellevue, a suburb of Seattle, on many weekends to share in family dinners and spent the holidays with us too. My grandmother had a quiet and sweet temperament and I appreciated spending time with her.

I loved my family and believed they would be around to share in all of my significant life experiences, well into my old age. They would be there for family vacations, my mom would share in my wedding planning, my father would be an inspiration to my children and my brother would regale us with his expert piano playing. As it turned out, none of it was to be. My mom became ill and was diagnosed with lung cancer and a brain tumor while I was 21 and away for several months visiting my dad. She was very sick when I got home, and when I got to her I felt very disconnected from the whole situation. Mom was in a lot of pain but didn't or couldn't communicate it very well. I didn't know how to help her. So, I would just sit there at her bedside, holding her hand with so much sadness in my heart, wishing there was something I could do. She died a just few months later.

Ken, who had never managed to create any sort of happiness for himself and wasn't able to find meaning in his life, was deeply affected by mom's passing. He committed suicide at age 22, a year and a half after my mom died. Ken and I had been living with mom until his death. I was coincidentally moving out that same week-end. After the shock of my mom and brother passing away in such a short amount of time, I thought to myself, "This absolutely means that dad will live to be at least 85 years old because there is no way he would die after I just lost mom and Ken." And yet my dad was already ill with a circulatory disease when I last went to visit and I had helped him through several leg amputations. I was terrified that my worst fears would come true as I learned more regarding the severity of his disease and further complications. I couldn't imagine life without my dad, and it left me feeling powerless.

Dad did die of these complications and a worn-out body about eighteen months after my mom passed away. I couldn't believe it! Then my grandmother, the last member of my family, became very ill and passed relatively quickly. At the time, I was living in Bellevue and had a full-time job at Nordstrom when I got the call that my grandmother was in the hospital with organ failure. I was able to get to the hospital one time and see her briefly. She wasn't even conscious and she passed away within the week. It was devastating to suddenly have every one of my family members gone.

The search for answers

Through each ordeal, I kept wondering why this was happening and what could possibly be the reason? Well-meaning friends and relatives would often say to me, "Everything happens for a reason, you know." And I believed them! They just never offered what the reasons might be. God knows I didn't have any answers. For myself, I was in survival mode just keeping up with things, feeling very afraid because my future was uncertain. I didn't know what I would do without my family.

As I wrestled with the sadness and confusion, I had a lot of trouble sleeping at night. I often got up and mentally rehashed each person's passing. Had I done enough for my family during their illnesses? I felt I was wholeheartedly there for my father, supporting him during his most difficult times. I was by his side for all of his many hospitalizations. On the other hand, I felt terrible guilt in my Mom's situation because I was in South America with my dad when she needed me the most.

And then there was Ken. He lived with mom and was working fulltime at a swim club and wasn't interested in sharing his feelings when I wanted to talk. It was really frustrating for me to not know where his head was at. When Mom died a couple of months later and Dad flew in from Chile, he invited Ken to come stay with him and work fulltime on his music. But he turned him down without a reason. Four months later my brother shot himself.

It was the worst feeling I had ever experienced to know my brother had felt so helpless. I never imagined he would do this. All I could think about was the countless times I had tried to coach him into finding joy in the little things in life. I remember telling him how happy it had made me to get new kitchen curtains for the tiny kitchen in what used to be our mom's house. I was so excited about it.

It was a long and traumatic three years. Why had everyone left so suddenly, not to mention traumatically? I didn't even know where to start finding answers. One story I considered was that they were all very sad and didn't want to be here anymore. But that didn't sound reasonable. I knew my brother was depressed. But I surely would have noticed this in my parents? Another spiritual story I considered was that on some level we were all part of a soul group who had agreed I would go it alone in this life for my own personal evolution and growth. This explanation felt better to me, even though I didn't know how the Universe worked and what each soul's path was. Being so out of control in that moment, I liked the idea that I was in control of who I would be in my future and that my evolution was inevitable.

Having reasons and answers, whether they are true or not, are a comfort. I think that is why we seek them out and cling to them. They are our attempt to explain the unexplainable. But for me there were no explanations. No reasons no matter who many times well-meaning people around me insisted there were. Just a solid blank wall. And with no real answers as to reasons, at first, it was a challenge to not be reactive and feel angry. But those feelings didn't feel good either. Strangely, it just didn't feel natural to me to feel angry at this situation. Sure, it would have been justified, but I had always innately felt there was more to this situation than could be explained or maybe ever known. The whole situation seemed too bizarre to actually be a bad thing. I know that may sound strange to say, but who loses their core family of four in three years for no *good* reason?

I have always had faith that what happens to me is ultimately for my highest good. I remember the most powerful experience I ever had with the Divine was when I was five years old and got pushed into a very deep swimming pool and was sinking to the bottom. I had the sensation that I was breathing and it was all happening in very slow motion. I wasn't afraid and I said to myself, "I wonder when my friend Anne Marie will jump in and save me." At that moment she did and I was saved.

I have always felt that that situation was a blessing and in the hands of a higher power. During the ordeal with my family, I had a sense that I was being held and protected from a higher source in a manner that was keeping me from devastation. But now that I was alone and didn't have my family around to help reinforce my identity, I began wondering *who am I anyway?* And what did I want to do from here? Who did I want to become? I switched from looking for answers and reasons and focused on issues I could have some control over.

Early on in life, I noticed that when I was feeling good, had positive expectations, and didn't allow negative or pessimistic thoughts to creep in, circumstances went the way I wanted them to. I also noticed that when I *didn't* keep a positive attitude, things could easily go haywire and I didn't get what I wanted. If I expected Mom to be mad at something I did, then she usually was. I never got what I wanted when I was adversarial with others and just wanted to argue. So, I made it a practice to go within and *feel* my best course of action, always choosing what felt the best and believing it would come to me.

No one had to teach me this. I just knew it innately. Frankly, I believe we all have an innate connection to knowing what's right for us. The problem is, people neglect to pay attention to what their intuition is telling them. I had become really good at listening to my heart and my gut and paying attention to the results. When my family passed away, I was still the person that expected life to go well. And now, more than ever, it was time to tap into the truth I knew about life. So I gave up looking for answers and reasons and determined I would reinvent myself, stay positive, and productively move on.

Life is going to happen to all of us. Some of it is what our dreams are made of and some of it isn't. There are many things in our lives that we can't control. We can't control others and we can't always control external circumstances. What we *can* control is our reaction and responses to the world around us. I have learned in my life that I get to choose how I think and in what manner I move forward, exclusive of everything that has happened to me. Over time, this has brought me a deep sense of wisdom and peace.

Sharon Ballantine is a parenting coach and founder of The Ballantine Parenting Institute, an online course for parents. Sharon has successfully raised three children and is the author of the book, *The Art of Blissful Parenting: Teaching Your Children How to Follow Their Internal Guidance.* Past work includes writing her own column for Beliefnet.com, "Parenting on Purpose," helping parents have a more easeful relationship with their kids. Sharon hosted her own weekly Internet TV Show with Conscious Evolution Media Network- The Sharon Ballantine TV Show. Her show featured a conversation with passionate spiritually minded guests. Sharon has been a guest speaker on many radio stations including Blog Talk Radio, Chat with Women, Hay House Radio and Conscious Evolution Media in Denver. She made a guest appearance on "New Day Northwest" live television in Seattle. Sharon lives in the Pacific Northwest with her husband Jay. You can see her educational videos on her YouTube channel, Sharon Ballantine. For blogs, tip videos, slideshows and "All Things Parenting" go to: www.SharonBallantine.com

Chapter 11

This is a popular belief in the spiritual community. Unfortunately, it dilutes the hard truth that being psychic is a learned skill, just like training to become a pianist or a plumber. There is a lot of confusion about the world of psychics and mediumship. In fact, most people don't even know there's a difference between the two. I have witnessed too many people armed with too little knowledge, development and ethics jump into readings for the public which can ultimately wound people, especially if they're grieving. Mediumship is often misunderstood and considered fraudulent by the general public simply because people with little knowledge are out there doing a job they're not trained to do.

MICHELE CUTLER

MEDIUMSHIP 101

I stared up at the Masonic Temple in Fort Collins, Colorado. It was historic, a bit eerie, yet a captivating building from the 1920s. I was so excited to be there that I was even a bit early.

Entering the building, my anticipation continued to grow because for the first time in my life I was about to experience a demonstration of mediumship by real professional mediums—people who wrote books and were well known. Of course, I hoped that my loved ones would come through, because I missed them and wanted to feel connected to them. But I was more excited just to witness the mediums' amazing abilities. Little did I know that a brief three years later, I would be in Maine attending my very first mediumship workshop with one of the mediums I saw in Colorado up on stage.

Because of my amateur fascination with all things metaphysical, I'd visited several psychics and mediums in my life. Some were amazing, some mediocre and some just plain awful. Many mentioned that I had psychic or intuitive abilities. But I dismissed the idea because I only knew some things about some people and some situations some of the time. To be a psychic didn't you have to know everything about everyone all the time? But then, after a big move to the east coast, I found a small holistic center near my new home and took classes on meditation, intuition and various spiritual topics. Seeking more, I bounced around to various Meetup groups until I met a woman, a medium, who told me I was a natural medium. (Whatever that was?) And that with training I could develop my mediumship. I didn't hesitate. I was in!

What's the difference?

There is a difference between being psychic and being a medium. First, we are all made up of energy and there is an energy field around us called the aura which holds all of our memories and experiences of our lifetime. A psychic blends with another's energy/aura and is able to perceive information about you and your experiences through a soul-to-soul connection. On the other hand, mediumship is the communication between a discarnate soul, the spirit person, and an incarnate soul, the medium. A medium receives information from a person that now resides in the spirit world. The medium passes on that information to the discarnate person's loved ones or whoever the recipient is. It is also a soul-to-soul and a mind-to-mind communication. All mediums are psychic, but all psychics aren't necessarily mediums.

Mediums have different specialties as well. For example there are three different types of mediumship: mental mediumship, healing mediumship and physical mediumship. Mental mediumship, which is what I study, is about proving the continuance of life after we leave this Earth plane supporting the theory that there is no death and that communication can take place with spirits in the spirit world. If we believe that the soul continues in the spirit world after death, it can bring comfort and understanding to those people who are grieving. It also can provide solace to those who fear death.

I have been taught evidence-based mediumship, meaning the medium has to come up with something more substantial than saying, "I have your grandmother here and she says she loves you and wants you to succeed in life." That is vague and doesn't validate that it is really your grandmother or anyone else in the spirit world. A trained evidential medium might say, for example, "I have a lady here who never learned to drive. She had five children. English was her second language and in her later years she taught the children in the neighborhood how to play the piano. She is here to speak with her granddaughter." This kind of clarity inspires confidence in the recipient and by the end of the communication the recipient might even feel her grandmother there as well!

A healing medium uses their mediumship to work with the spirit world to provide healing to the recipient during a light altered state or a trance. Physical mediumship is when a medium enables a physical phenomenon to occur, such as the production of ectoplasm—a supernatural viscous substance that is supposed to exude from the body of a medium during a spiritualistic trance and form the material for the manifestation of spirits. Physical mediumship is very rare these days and there is a lot of fraud associated with it. In fact, mediumship institutions such as the Arthur Findlay College only allow physical mediumship in a room dimly lit, not complete darkness, and it must be recorded and/or night vision goggles allowed to prevent deceit.

Why you need training

Often I hear comments such as "Do you see anyone around me?" or "If you are psychic, you would have known that." These two statements alone reveal how people have a plethora of misunderstandings about the work psychics and mediums do. People unfamiliar with the practice of mediumship sometimes think that mediums walk around seeing spirits or "dead people" everywhere (as in The Sixth Sense). They think spirits wake us up all hours of the night and that they are always asking us to give random messages to people. If this was the way I experienced it I would not study or practice mediumship! It would be a nerve racking, scary and just a crazy way to live.

As I started to develop my mediumship, it became apparent that I didn't have to have my connection to the spirit world turned on all the time. Yes, it's an exciting shiny new penny when we first tap into our abilities. But I don't walk around reading everyone I see and talking to all of their deceased loved ones. So no worries there! You can have a conversation with me without me telling you that your deceased mother wants you to eat more vegetables. I have learned to only connect when I am working.

There are many reasons why professional training is so vitally necessary. Without proper training, mediums new to their abilities can connect with the spirit world and get a few pieces of information about the person. But if they don't hone their mediumship skills, they can shift to reading the recipient psychically and not even know it. They might go back and forth, mediumship then psychic then mediumship. This isn't a problem if you're trained to be aware of the difference. Then you can say, "You need to know I received that information psychically from you. Ah, wait a minute. Now I'm picking up your mom and she's saying …"

That's okay. But if the sitter thinks it's mom talking to her the whole time and the medium is actually psychically reading her, saying "Mom says _____," it's not true and it shouldn't be represented that way. And who knows? You might meet the sitter's mom in the spirit world again someday and you don't want her asking, "Why did you tell my daughter I said _____? I didn't say that and she ruined her life because she believed I said it." I would not want to have that conversation, even in the spirit world!

Boundaries and ethics should be observed. For example, you shouldn't do "ambush readings," meaning you can't go up to someone in the grocery store and say, "Do you have a father in the spirit world?"

This can cause problems for the medium and the recipient. It can be an unwelcomed interaction and it can really be traumatic for people to be approached like this. It can open up old wounds and leave someone in more pain and confusion than before.

Another consideration is we all have unconscious bias. Untrained mediums might not understand this concept and can get inappropriately critical or judgmental in a reading. Or they can dismiss information because their personal experience creates a bias against believing the information they're getting. They make assumptions. For instance, if a reader sees a lady with a flowery dress and an apron who loves to bake they assume, "Oh, this must be grandmother." Well, today grandma might have tattoos and ride a Harley. But through our unconscious bias we might be confused by grandma riding a Harley and not admit the information. So, it is about really surrendering to the information coming through and not allowing the left brain to analyze it.

In a simplistic example, I remember one time I made a contact with a lady who kept showing me a bike. It felt very significant, and I said, "She rode her bike every day. She rode it into town. She rode it everywhere." It was strange to me, being from the US, for a bike to be the main source of transportation. But much later when I traveled to the Netherlands I found that the large majority of people there ride their bikes everywhere. If I hadn't been trained to trust the spirit world to bring forth important evidence, I could have ignored important evidence coming through.

Some of the pain an untrained medium can cause is from inflicting dogma or old belief systems or even new belief systems onto their clients. For example, I have heard that after a spirit has come through offering an apology to a recipient that some mediums tell the recipient that they must forgive the spirit or that soul can't move on or evolve in the spirit world. In my humble opinion, this is just plain garbage and can be hurtful to the recipient because it puts the responsibility of someone's soul growth on their very human plate.

Untrained mediums can also be insensitive and say things that are inappropriate. I was once in a group of students doing an exercise for a class. A student was to bring forth a contact for the group, then bring forth evidence and determine who the contact belonged too. The student being the medium said, "I have a baby here." We all looked at each other and no one in the group could identify the baby. Frustrated the medium said, "Have any of you miscarried or aborted a child?" I couldn't believe the bluntness of her question. I was literally at a loss for words and I wished I had brought it to the attention of the tutor so he could have coached her. When working with the public, we must find ways to bring forth our evidence in a softer or more compassionate way. For example, she could have said something like "a child who never touched the earth."

It is important to consider that there is often a grieving human being sitting in front of you who is in pain from their loss and fearful they will never see their loved one again. As mediums, we must learn how to positively interact with our recipients and hold in mind that there is a sacredness to this work and that we are serving the spirit world and humanity.

Growing as a medium

Recognizing when you have a contact with the spirit world is different for everyone. When I have a link or a contact with the spirit world I literally feel like there is someone standing next to me usually off my right shoulder. The best way I can describe what I feel is that it feels similar to when someone comes too close to you, maybe when you're standing in line somewhere and you can feel that they have stepped too close into your space. When I recognize that feeling, I usually instantly know if it is a man or a woman and as soon as I say "I have a man" more information comes through in my mind in many different ways. Sometimes I see pictures, get feelings or just know information which is scary as I know and speak at the same time. So sometimes I'm not sure what is coming out of my mouth as I say it. On the other hand when I tap into reading someone psychically I, for one, don't have that feeling of someone standing there. Instead, I almost feel a connection from my center like my soul is reaching out to their soul.

It's not an easy journey training in mediumship. Mistakes are inevitable, but we often become fearful of making errors. Not letting your fear hinder your mediumship is key. And yet looking at why we get the information wrong is also where our own personal growth comes from. I remember working with another student in a mediumship exercise. I had brought through my partner's grandmother with some solid evidence. But then the information I started getting generated a few "no's." Arg! The dreaded NO! My tutor walked me through the information I had received and I made a few more statements. Maybe true statements, but not the core pieces or the healing pieces. In frustration, I sat back and suddenly realized, "There is nobody there during the holidays." And my tutor replied, "Yes. She's lonely. And you didn't want to feel loneliness. So you kept dodging and going around the emotion and wouldn't allow yourself to feel it and then communicate it."

I had to sit with that one. And it was incredibly helpful in prompting me to start recognizing that I have locked up many of my emotions from childhood. And if I don't know how to feel a certain emotion, how will I recognize it when it comes from a person in the Spirit World? This isn't an easy process to say the least. Sometimes it feels as though you are putting yourself through the blender. But this realization started a long journey of awareness and healing pieces of my own past so I could ultimately be vulnerable and feel emotion when working with other's loved ones that had passed to the Spirit World.

The other thing that training and years of practice build is trust. Trust that the spirit world is giving you accurate information. Sometimes you think you get it wrong when you actually have it right. I was doing a small expo and had a lady sit down for a reading. I felt I had a man and I saw a school bus. I felt that there was some type of ritual around this school bus with her children. She said no, no, no. So finally I let him go and made a couple other contacts she could understand. The next day, she came back to the expo to let me know that she remembered the man and the school bus. There was a neighbor down the street that used to honk and wave to her and her children every morning while they waited for the school bus. Sometime the sitter just doesn't remember the information. So, I just leave the information with them and maybe someday it will make sense to them.

I hope, writing all this, that you can understand a little bit better now how important it is not to take psychic abilities and psychic work and mediumship lightly. Is everyone psychic like the saying goes? Well, I think all humans have the capacity for psychic sensitivity to a greater or lesser degree. But even if you're extremely sensitive and easily pick up information from the Spirit World and from the energetic auras of people around you that doesn't mean you're ready and capable of working as a professional.

Another part of the problem is that there is a limited support system here in the US for developing mediums. There is definitely more guidance today than in the past with online opportunities and tutors coming from around the world to teach here in the US and some established and new spiritualist centers/churches. In the UK, there are more spiritualist churches which have programs to develop mediums and colleges that support mediumship development and opportunities to practice their skills through student demonstration nights and probationary mediums programs.

Bottom line, if you have the gift, wonderful. Embrace it. Approach it as the important craft that it is. Give it the years of study it deserves and requires. Practice, practice, practice! This is the imperative for development. All the same, I wish there were karaoke nights for mediums!

Michele Cutler has been studying mediumship and serving the spirit world and says "it's an honor." She has been fortunate enough to study abroad at the Arthur Findlay College in Stansted, England and the College of Psychic Studies in London. She continues her studies enjoying courses at The Journey Within in New Jersey. She credits her knowledge of mediumship to the amazing tutors that she has had the privileges to study under. Her 27+ years working for a major airline has allowed her to pursue her dreams due to her flexible schedule, finishing her education with a BS in Natural Resources followed by a Master's in Management Practice. She has had great opportunities to work and volunteer for many non-profits, from disaster relief for animals to conservation groups. Her passion comes from teaching and inspiring people in many different ways. Michele enjoys spending time with her husband, Ted, getting out into nature, traveling the world and finding ancestors through genealogy. They have a house full of dogs and cats and their horses are nearby. Michele's dream is to one day operate and/or own a retreat center where self-awareness and self-development are the cornerstone of people's transformations. Where all are welcome to become their best self. For more information: www.michelewalksthepath.com

Chapter 12

In Eastern philosophy, the ego has been the subject of spiritual teachings for a very long time, more recently becoming a hot topic in Western culture with the rise of the New Age movement. It is commonly thought that the ego is bad and to blame for all our negative aspects and should be dissolved, transcended or even killed. Unfortunately, this way of thinking allows us to be unaccountable and deny responsibility for our actions. What a difference realizing that our egos are our lifelong companions, and that if we deny any aspects, good or bad, we create further separation within, making it difficult to love and accept ourselves. Realizing we are responsible for shaping our egos enables us to use the ego as an asset rather than it being an impediment to our journey.

Parri Ulrich

Is Ego The Enemy?

Ego. Such a small word to encapsulate something that is so incredibly great and powerful, just like the Wizard of Oz. But perhaps all is not as it seems. Let's pull back the curtain and have a peek.

What is the ego? In Latin, ego simply means "I." The Oxford Dictionary of English defines it as a person's sense of self-esteem or self-importance. Dictionary.com says it is the "I" or self of any person; a person as thinking, feeling, and willing, and distinguishing itself from the selves of others and from objects of its thought.

But start a conversation with anyone about ego, and you will soon hear that it has come to encompass and even exemplify traits such as conceit, arrogance, vanity, narcissism, selfishness, self-importance and so on. We *accuse* one of having a big ego, rather than celebrating the strength of their individuality. Obviously the consensus is that the ego is indeed unwanted and perhaps even beyond redemption. Still, why has it garnered such an enormous amount of negative publicity? Why are so many, from the novice to great spiritual teachers such as Eckhart Tolle, Adyashanti and Deepak Chopra, to name only a few, so eager to paint the ego with such an unflattering brush, encouraging transcendence from same?

Somehow over the years, the ego has become representative of all things undesirable. When we take a step back, we begin to see how very complex and vast the ego and our interpretation of it really is. It is convenient and even soothing to accept the much-lauded idea of "Ego is the Enemy," as it gives us a place to lay the blame for all the things we don't wish to own. It is easy to jump on the bandwagon of all the popular teachings on this subject, as this allows us to continue the story that we still don't get it—that we're still imperfect.

If the road to wholeness and enlightenment is paved in self-love, how do we even begin to take the first steps towards that when we believe that we are intrinsically flawed? That we have something that needs to be transcended, dissolved or put aside? What if we have it all wrong? What if the very thing that we are trying to escape is actually our greatest teacher, our biggest defender?

My own ego journey

I own a bed & breakfast just outside of Victoria, BC, Canada, and most of the guests attend neurofeedback training at a nearby Institute—a week of intense introspection and personal transformation. They come from around the world, ranging in age, ethnic diversity, religious backgrounds, occupations and spiritual knowledge. A common goal of many is to get rid of or transcend their ego. They speak of it as if it were the only obstacle in the way of their enlightenment, their success and their happiness.

When I attended this training in 2011, I held the same view. I was in the midst of a marital breakdown, my ego matched only by that of my husband. The battles were fierce, ranging from monetary issues to jealousy to our children—the subject less important than the need to be right. Our competitive natures were in their glory duking it out, and while our egos ran the show, there was no compromise. There could, after all, only be one winner in any war.

Thus, our marriage came to a fiery demise, leaving no-one unscathed and no winners at all. Not only were we devastated as our dreams of a white picket fence and rocking chairs on the porch went up in flames, worse still was that we had failed our children, ripping their very foundation out from under them, the impact reverberating deeply for many years to come. Of course, I blamed our egos for this. If only we could have set them aside and worked together towards a solution! Neither of us were yet capable of that, believing that the other was to blame with their fixed ideas and opinions. While there was some validity to that, I also have since come to thank our egos. For it was in the void, the sorrow, the surrender that we were able to find our deeper truths, buried beneath layers of false beliefs and egoic masks.

The noble ego

In the place of surrender, there is no ego. When I was curled up in the fetal position, sobbing in the bathtub, my ego was nowhere to be found. "Ego is the enemy" – *hmmmm*. I think in some cases that the ego may be the saviour, may be that very thing that helps us put one foot in front of the other until such a time where we are able to do that for ourselves. When we are taken to our knees, it is very difficult to push forward, and what enables us to do that is our ego. Our ego is not just the bad guy, the fall guy, the one who gets in the way of our enlightenment and all of the other stories we tell ourselves, it is also our knight in perhaps not-so-shining armor, helping us to take the next step when we're not ready, when we're really not feeling it.

Our ego is created in separation, in the separation from what we think we are and the image we think we need to present to the world. However, our ego is also our faithful guardian. It's our bodyguard, ready to take all the hits to protect the vulnerable, the open-hearted— the us that wouldn't be able to withstand the anger, blame or other negative emotions and accusations being directed towards us. For me, when life hit hard in the fallout from my divorce and I really didn't know how I was going to make it through the day, it was my ego that got me up, got me out, pushed me through the motions and provided a false front to the world so that my broken pieces had time to reassemble.

But this noble version of the ego does not fit with most of the teachings around the ego. Indeed, it has been dragged out like a sacrificial lamb as an offering for our atonement. For it is in the places that we find lacking in ourselves, where we believe we are less than perfect (and to show that to the world would be a threat to our very survival), this is how and where the ego takes shape. It is in the separation from the truth of our perfection that the need for ego presents yet another mask. But what if we were to embrace our ego? To have gratitude for all the ways that it not only shows up in our lives, but stands for us, sovereign, when we are anything but that?

What if we took responsibility and ownership of our ego, recognizing that it is our desire to express ourselves, to be seen by the outer world as we wish to be seen, that creates the form, and that we can consciously choose to shape the ego in whatever way we wish?

Part of my role at the bed & breakfast is to hold and even create space for the guests as they go through their training. Much of the work they do is centered around identifying and forgiving people and situations that are holding them back or causing them distress in some way. This journey into Pandora's box often leaves them feeling extremely vulnerable as they do the work to peel back the layers that years of conditioning and false beliefs have created. There is a phenomenon which often occurs on the third day of training, where the ego rises within them in various ways, such as telling them they're not "doing it right," that the training is a waste of money and time, that they will never "get" it. It even sometimes triggers physical symptoms such as fatigue or illness.

I remember when I was doing the training that the facilitator spoke of day three, telling us that the ego wants to keep us small and asleep and is threatened by our efforts to dissolve it through the forgiveness work we were doing. At that time in my life, and for many subsequent years, I held that as a truth. Shortly after I bought the B&B, a young girl came down on Day 3 for breakfast and cried the entire meal, not eating a bite. As I am a lover of crystals and believe they have healing energy, I gave her a piece of rose quartz for self-love. The next training, two boys were having difficulty sleeping, so I gave them howlite to put under their pillows. From that point forward, I offered everyone a crystal gifting on Day 3 to assist them in their week and would preface it with a brief speech about the ego, very similar to that which I had heard years before.

About a year and a half ago, as the words were passing my lips, something inside me vehemently protested. I am not sure at what precise moment my beliefs shifted from left to right, but I found myself struggling to get through my well-rehearsed spiel. I felt completely liberated from the need to do anything with my ego, except perhaps to consciously shape it into alignment with my truth, and to articulate its expression in the world. Love and gratitude surged through me for all the parts and pieces that hid in the shadow of my ego, afraid to be seen by others, and for my ego itself, for bearing the weight of all of the judgements, guilt, shame, anger, etc. directed at it over the years. My ego and I were set free—or so I thought.

Layers of identity

I recently returned from my seventh journey to Teotihuacan in Mexico. In the past, these journeys had not only revealed many aspects of my character to me, as well as wounds that were available to be healed, but also provided a building of strength, joy, energy and heightened awareness of my true nature. This journey seemed on track to follow that course until a deep childhood wound of being unseen and unheard as if I didn't matter was triggered within me on the night before our last day.

Feelings of hurt, embarrassment, confusion and anger all came bubbling forth, my almost 50-year old self transported back to a much earlier time in my childhood, with pitstops along the way. Images of similar incidents flashed through my mind like a kaleidoscope of pain,

116

and the accompanying feelings coursed through my veins. I blinked back the tears, willed the flaming heat to leave my face, and sat silently waiting for the evening session to wrap up. I headed for my room, wanting to isolate with my pain, but a couple of friends came to check on me. Sobs wracked my body, and tears soaked my friend's shoulder as the intensity of the withheld emotions was released. As my breathing returned to normal, I assured them that I'd be fine after a good night's sleep.

The next morning, we set out for Tetitla, the "Place of the Eagles," which is considered by many to be the most transformative of all the places we visit during the week. Not only was that not the case for me this time, but the wound from the previous evening was triggered even more strongly. Anger took the forefront, with all the previous day's emotions close behind. For a moment I considered foregoing the finale of the journey—the Pyramid of the Sun. But I quickly resolved that I was not going to let this ruin my experience. We walked to the pyramid grounds, then stopped for a snack and restroom break before entering the gates. I closed my eyes and placed my hand on a nearby pepper tree, asking for support to get me through the day.

Immediately I heard, "Don't be silly. It's just a branch!" and got a visual of a tree that has been pruned, and next to the cut is where the new growth appears. I laughed out loud and felt an immediate wave of relief wash over me. I then heard, "And let go of that story!" I shook my head at my brief but powerful descent into a hell of my own creation, or that of my ego. How humbling to be handed such a powerful reminder that as knowledgeable and conscious as we may be, we are still as vulnerable as our deepest unhealed wound!

Always more

Over the past several weeks, I have had many conversations with many people regarding the ego. I have read articles, watched YouTube videos, poked and prodded my loved ones for their thoughts/opinions, and to quote Albert Einstein, "The more I learn, the more I realize how much I don't know."

The ego is too vast, too complex and too individually personal to understand on more than a cursory level. Ego is everything (and nothing). It is experienced in pieces. And when you talk about the ego, that is emulated in the conversation. The further I delved, the more elusive it became, like trying to grasp the light, feeling a bit of warmth for a moment, but nothing that I could truly hold on to as an absolute.

I wonder if L. Frank Baum had similar thoughts when he wrote *The Wonderful Wizard of Oz* back in 1900? Not only could you say that the ego is depicted by "Oz, the great and terrible," but also every other character representing its many faces, from the Lion, the Scarecrow and the Tinman to all of the witches, both good and wicked, to the Munchkins, the flying monkeys, even Auntie Em, Uncle Henry and Toto! Each character portrays aspects of our ego-self, from the most benevolent to the parts of us that feel as if we are not brave enough, smart enough, not worthy of love—highlighting what we think we need and what we lack in order to be perfect.

Left unconscious, these aspects can hinder our journey. But through the light of awareness they can become our greatest allies. Though it may not have been the intended premise behind the story, what a brilliant illustration of the all-encompassing nature of the ego it is. Like the road to Oz, life is filled with many difficult experiences, often putting us in situations where we feel scared to proceed on our own or feel that we need to "armor up" in order to do so.

Thankfully, we have our ego to hold our hand and to fight our battles, allowing us to continue on our path. Set free from the role of the enemy, our ego, aligned with our truth and our awareness, can help us to do magnificent things and reach people on an unprecedented level. No ruby slippers required!

Parri Ulrich is an alternative healing practitioner, owner of Markham House Bed & Breakfast on Vancouver Island in British Columbia, Canada, and the mom of three beautiful children. Parri's journey through life and quest for spiritual knowledge have brought her to many places, allowing her to experience many different founts of wisdom, including the traditional Toltec teachings of Mexico and Teotihuacan, and the alpha brainwave neurofeedback training facilitated by the Biocybernaut Institute. Her passion and desire to help people reconnect to their true divine nature has led her to learn many modalities, including Reconnective Healing and The Reconnection, the Hartman Approach to Hypnotherapy, Craniosacral Therapy, Intuitive Chakra Therapy, and Angel Empowerment Practitioner. Parri is in the process of building a retreat and workshop center, with the intention of creating a sacred space for healing and transformation, as well as group gatherings. For more information: www.reconnect4life.com

Chapter 13

Being all full of words and not taking action is one of my biggest points of frustration. This famous meme was written by Anne Herbert on a placemat in Sausalito, California in 1982, and she wrote a book about people's acts of kindness in 1993. The foundation of the saying is about *doing*—that you have to get down in the trenches and get your hands dirty to get things done to help people. Nowadays people like to promote this saying, but even in the spiritual community most people seem to be just doing the very minimal amount of actual practice so that they look good and can brag to their friends on social media. I find this deeply saddening.

Morgan D. Hartt

Kindness Is Love In Work Boots

Growing up autistic while having an angry mother created challenges and hurdles I still deal with today. I have Asperger's, a form of autism, also referred to as Autistic Spectrum Disorder or ASD. It was hard to tell me a lot of times from any other kid, except I have more issues with learning and understanding social skills and I'm not good at reading facial cues. This coupled with being bullied in school, from elementary to middle school to high school, became my trauma, shaping me again and again into a person that I did not like—an angry person, quick to explode, focusing on the latest bad event of the moment. And because I understood the impact of when I did get angry, I felt horrible about it. To see the pain in another person's eyes and realize that I had caused it is not something I ever will be comfortable with.

I got to see the trauma anger inflicts firsthand as my mother would lash out at people. How that anger would cause a ripple effect, how it would cause ongoing trauma. Sometimes as a kid it was like watching things in slow-motion, like some slow-motion scene of a car wreck on TV. When it happened in a restaurant or store, I could visibly see, at times, the demeanor of the place change. I remember time and again when some waitress or server would make a mistake on a dinner order, yelling was sure to follow. And, just like a stone skipping across the pond leaving ripple after ripple as it touches down again and again, the negative effects would spread out through the room.

Let me tell you, you do learn what you live. Like my mother, I had low coping skills, low social skills and would get angry as my default "go to" emotional state. And when you get angry the higher brain functions shut down. You can feel it happening. You lose control, your

121

ability to plan goes away, you lose your ability to think, you lose fluid intelligence, and, worst of all, your ability to problem solve is lost.

But you don't have to be angry to have a negative impact on others and the world around you. Sometimes an even more devastating action is indifference and not caring. With anger at least there is an exchange of energy. It may be negative energy. It may be damaging. But at least there is an exchange—something is happening between people. Both people are visible and acknowledged. There's engagement. But indifference? Indifference means the people around you are so insignificant that they hardly even exist. And hard as it may seem to believe, sometimes I think that indifference and half-hearted measures are the cruelest cut of all.

Kindness and giving are seen as hugely important in both Christian and spiritual communities. Kindness is a virtue. Giving is better than receiving. And yet the amount of lip service kindness and giving get is astonishing. You see the problem from church to church and from non-profit to non-profit. Churches that have a Sacred Saturday once a year where members donate time to the community, charities that do a charity event only occasionally, and neither want to show you how much they actually give and receive.

There is this emphasis on "me me me" in the spiritual community. *My* learning, *my* enlightenment, *my* manifestations, *my* issues, *my* problems. Everybody seems to be into the quick fix. Tune into my show! Come to my seminar! Reach nirvana over the weekend! There's all too often the feeling that problems—especially community problems like homelessness and hunger, drug addiction, depression and suicide—have been sent off to some committee. And love dies in committee.

So many people talk about doing something, so few take real action. It's like signing an online petition has replaced volunteer work and getting our hands dirty. (Three dollars worth of God.) Instead of a YouTube video or a Facebook ad, how much more meaningful would it be to SEE that celebrity, host, person, spiritual teacher, DOING charity work, even just once a month? When all is said and done, much is said and little is done. My frustration has been huge within the spiritual and nonprofit world.

Choosing change

When I was 14 years old, I chose to look my anger in the face and make a choice to be different, to be a better me than I was yesterday. I started volunteering at soup kitchens. Then I started dropping off food to homeless camps, falling in love with helping and finding it amazingly rewarding. The way a person's eyes would light up with just a sandwich or a warm meal, and how very thankful they were! It was humbling, because here I had a roof over my head and though things were far from perfect, I still had so much. Then to see the gratitude and to be thanked again and again, sometimes for such little things …

As a volunteer, I noticed that, just like waves of anger, there could be waves of love. I could see the love from the volunteers, the people who came in early at three and four in the morning to prep the food for the soup kitchens. I loved coming in first thing in the morning and turning on the lights, starting the processes of the day. Realizing we would serve over 1,200 meals that day and that some part of every one of those meals was worked on by me—man, that felt great! I saw and felt the impact. And that amazing feeling, that wonderful feeling of helping another human being, was such a gift to me. And how empowering it was knowing that no matter where I might be emotionally or mentally I could help my fellow man! That got me to recommit time and time again to contributing and doing good. In the year 2000 the movie *Pay It Forward* was released, and a quiet movement that had been going on for years suddenly gained international attention. I had never thought of kindness/love on such a grand scale and I was stunned! That coupled with the power of the internet. Wow! Since then there have been thousands of kindness and love nonprofits that have opened. For myself, I embraced the *Pay It Forward* movement in simple ways, paying for people's food and coffee behind me in line at a restaurant. Putting money in expired parking meters. Putting out my neighbor's garbage cans. Quietly and behind the scenes, I volunteered to be part of the solution.

Today you can find me volunteering, normally daily. I'm even taking steps to start a nonprofit outreach to feed the hungry, bringing hope and showing kindness in action. The charity system I am working on is setup to be duplicated by churches and charity groups worldwide, allowing the program to grow and become more. The charity system will allow each group to start their own charity, allowing each to work together in groups or individually with an active social media campaign to help spread and grow the ideas. Together we will be the change we wish to see!

Taking action

What if you could give, even just a little bit? What if you could also inspire others in the process? It is the next logical step in giving/volunteering to make it public. Today I can pay for someone's groceries, shoot the scene with my phone and put it on social media—not to show off or try to impress people with how good I am, but to inspire others with a vision of how easy and rewarding it is helping people in need. How wonderful it would be to see your pastor or minister giving to those in need! Or your neighbor! Or your children! Each of us can be a bright light in someone's day, creating ripples of love and kindness across this world. It is a way to engage humanity in a positive way.

I started out as an advocate for kindness and love in my teens. Today, at almost 50, I am even more committed to doing just that and so much more, believing that we can change the world with one kind act of love at a time.

I do my best to be kind, and that equals loving. I strive to do that in and through action, not talk. I am not saying I have this down. No not at all. Choosing kindness instead of anger, for me it is an everyday battle with myself—often many times a day. Just today I found myself getting angry about someone misunderstanding me, which is a trigger point for me. I had to take several deep breathes, relax and realize that the person was drawing a conclusion about me, but entirely from their own very limited life experiences.

I choose to be kind. Sometimes it is truly a challenge for me to be giving and not just angry. But through acts of kindness, I have become less depressed, more engaged with life and a better, more well-rounded person. I am able to look on the world with kinder eyes, to see ways to help others I could not see before. And that has changed me. My frustration has decreased and I have more resources than ever today! I have met people that I never would have met any other way, and I make an effort every day to share positivity on social media. Yes, these are all small things, but they sure add up over a decade or more.

What I can say? It gets easier with time and practice.

Some of the other things I do sometimes is take long breaks from negative news, going so far as to only seek positive news and information. I focus on finding positive news posts/memes and sharing those, doing my best to remind myself and other people of hope, love and gratitude, committing to being a force of positive change.

How do we change the world? We change it with kindness, giving and love. And how do we put that into action? One person, one moment at a time. As I transmute my anger into love via kindness, I've realized that, "Kindness is just love with its work boots on."

Morgan D. Hartt started volunteering at a young age, seeing it as an answer to a personal problem with depression after being abused at home and bullied at school. "It's hard to be depressed when you are helping others!" he says. A passionate believer in the Law of Attraction, he is currently preparing to launch a non-profit organization designed to help prevent and fight nonprofit fraud. Morgan has studied Neuro Linguistic Programming (NLP), Emotional Freedom Technique (EFT), and applies these to positive thinking and the Law of Attraction through his work as a coach at CheeringForYou.com. Morgan has worked and consulted in such diverse fields as the legal and medical research professions, computer science, chemistry, personal and business coaching, insurance and real estate. He also currently works with many nonprofits as both volunteer and as a active board member. He can be reached at: www.CheeringForYou.com

Chapter 14

*Find
the goddess
within*

Like   Comment   Share

"Finding the goddess within" all too easily turns into a surface level, glamorous, trendy exploration of the feminine. Having been in functional research of the Divine Feminine for over three decades, my experience tells me that waking the goddess within has little to do with outward appearance and more crucially to do with an awakening, a reverence, an intimate engagement with aspects and energies that've been so sublimated by the patriarchy, the archeological dig requires absolute presence and a sensitive touch. There's also been a certain popular level of "goddess" engagement that resonates as anti-male, and even more - finding the "warrior" within. Vilifying the masculine feels dangerous and irresponsible to me. Becoming the masculinized warrior goddess, equally so. Waking the Goddess within, so she may then inform and collaborate with a healthy masculine is the actual aspiration, and is anything but surface. Verily, her well runs infinitely deep.

Kate Rodger, Ph.D.

I, Goddess

She said we needed to do battle. Cloaked in a raven, sharp-edged, not-quite-Armani-pantsuit, she approached the podium at the ready, with a steel gaze and a taut jaw. The keynote speaker of this charity awards luncheon gripped the dais in a moment of stalwart feminist glory, spot-lit, before an ovation of admiring women and their allies silently crying out *Inspire us! Guide us! Give us the next indicated step!* while they applauded.

The crowd settled, and the editor of *Ms.* magazine began to speak. The recipe she poured forth to this room of game-changers, public servants, and endowing philanthropists was nothing short of a flashback to what must have been a clarion call in the 1970s.

But the year was 2012.

I couldn't believe my ears, I couldn't believe my eyes. With a rush of disbelief almost bordering on anxiety, I withdrew from the cheering crowd to catch my breath and scan the high-end room at the Beverly Hills Hotel. What this influencer, this powerfully positioned warrior woman—this modern-day High Priestess—was asserting sounded like a women's liberation call to arms from my childhood.

Her talk pitted "us" against "them," enumerating and expanding upon bullet points of grievances, outrage, and afflictions. We and all the causes we believed in were victims and "they," were oppressors. With articulate ammunition, she entreated the sisterhood and all sympathetic cohorts to mobilize against the opposition.

My skin was crawling, my heart racing as tears welled in my eyes. The whole room melted away while an aching sense of grief rose within me. What was being woven here? What ideologies were being amplified, subscribed-to, and concretized? Where was the steady voice of the contemporary priestess—a dynamic woman who understands the vitalizing force of the holy feminine, who is rooted deeply in a conversation of collaboration, possibility, and interdependence? Why was the executive editor of *Ms.* not speaking from the native resonance and intelligence of the Feminine, if, indeed, She is on the Rise?

An incredulous fire burned through my system.

Mind you, it's not that the underlying intent of her talking points was faulty. I absolutely understood where she was coming from. Personally and not so privately, I've traveled through the decades of my life with an evolving conversation about the poisonous patriarchy. Here, though, right now, a silver-plated and outdated attitude of division and antipathy was being served-up to a multitude of aspiring women, activists, and donors. It was surreal! How could this face of feminism be so insidiously pitching a social design manufactured by the barbarous side of the masculine?

This contemporary woman, following in the footsteps of women who came before—glorious, valiant women who'd carved out a path for humanity to traverse and grow from, birthing metamorphic solutions—this present-day face of feminism was dogmatically imparting a plan of action more akin to the muddled lens of the obsolete Patriarchy: playing that same game, rather than birthing a new reality. Angry, judgmental, corrosive and ultimately hierarchical.

I forever bow to the countless revolutionary women on whose shoulders we stand, the ones who penetrated the enmeshed fraternal jungle with their unrelenting insight, unstoppable passion, and keen-edged machetes. Uncontestably, these women were the fully embodied Goddesses of their day, and I kiss the ground these chivalrous priestesses walked upon. And yet, forty years (give or take) have passed.

Now is not then

The days of becoming like men in order to achieve anything are over. I've used countless hours, days, and years assisting women raised by feminists to extricate themselves from their rusted and suffocating masculinized armor, myself included. In all of this dismantling, what have we women been liberated to? Ostensibly, the "goddess within."

Oh, dear! Really? The "goddess within?"

There's another catch-phrase currently trending the realms of spiritual seekers along with talk of the Goddess: "Divine Feminine." And word on the Aquarian streets is *She is Rising*.

"Divine Feminine . . . Goddess Within." Uh . . . what exactly is that?

Since roughly 2002 I've been in intentional inquiry regarding the energetics of the feminine, and in all of my research I've gleaned that essential understanding of the "Goddess" and what we're calling the "Divine Feminine" *must* be informed at the level of energetics, the way all of life is.

Certainly, I know what the *opposite* of the feminine energetic is.

Raised in a conservative, hard-working, achievement-oriented Irish Catholic family with two aspiring Jesuit brothers, my mother wired me with an unwavering sense of masculine independence. "I am raising you," she pointedly said, waving her finger at twelve-year-old me, "so that you will *never* be dependent on a man." Having lost her father at the age of 15, my mama was survival-oriented and determined to equip her daughter with a self-sufficient operating system, as I sprouted forth into the big-wide world.

This was the seventies, at the height of the Feminist Movement, when Rosie the Riveter was an emblematic Shero with her "We can do it!" maxim. Under her auspices we rallied (and muscled) our way to fulfilling a vision of equality that involved maneuvering like the men in power so that we might taste this suddenly attainable elixir. The sexual revolution in full swing, women joined the work force, and began to, yes, shatter glass ceilings.

But what, precisely, was the infrastructure that engineered those glass ceilings?

Why, the Patriarchy, of course—a legendary paradigm architected mostly by men, concretized with systemic hierarchy and fueled by the lure of acquisition, achievement, and recognition. *To see and be seen! To own and control!* This mantra, as we well know, has succeeded in creating contemporary civilization by utilizing the strategies of domestication, supremacism, and social stratification, not to mention domination of our living planet. An unhinged, destructive, masculine energetic run amok.

Women and men alike have been acculturated to believe in this construct, to believe that in order to succeed in life we must operate like men. In order to be valid, we must compete. In order to be seen, we must accomplish. In order to be heard, we must out-smart, one-up, or bully our way to the top, resolute in fighting the good fight.

Divide and conquer.

I don't know about you, but personally, I'm exhausted by this lopsided, devastating approach to living. Which is why, back in 2002, I needed to find some relief from the suffocating constructs of my world. It was from this exhausted/inspired place that I set out to discover another way to be and function—to understand Life's Operating System via the lens of energetics, and to understand the feminine energetic way of being and showing up in the world.

For energy itself has no agenda. And energy picks no favorites. The only thing energy does is express itself.

A deep dive

Throughout my years and various avenues of female study, I've encountered many matri-centric women and goddess-allied groups who mused soulfully over a dream of mitigating the virulent patriarchy by bringing back the good 'ol days when women ruled the world. A remarkable number of women I've intersected with via my own shero's journey were deeply cut with an anti-male groove, propagating visions of a flipped hierarchy and consecrated she-dogma. Like *Ms.* magazine's editorial leader, so many women I met seemed to be mimicking the very men they rallied against. Which was super confusing, and it totally turned me off.

With no immediate frame of reference for what the Divine Feminine even was, I slipped into the dark unknown of my own anarchy and an intimate exploration of all things femmé. I suspected the grail I was looking for lay in something wordless and primordial, ungraspable, dark and dank—the in-between-the-sounds place, the before-the-before.

Already acquainted with the Sumerian, Akkadian, and Egyptian goddesses Inanna, Ishtar and Isis, and having explicitly explored the sensual goddess within myself during my roaring twenties, I aimed to understand foundational feminine intelligence, resonance, and functionality.

I meditated and conversed with the Magdalene, Guinevere, Aphrodite, and Lilith - each feminine icon providing pinnacle insights, invitations, and directives. Then along came the Hawaiian Goddess Pelé, who taught me about the Holy Blaze and practical use of feminine anger. It was Madame Pelé who helped me see that fires and the passion that fuels those flames can birth new realities—particularly when the quantum field is ignited with righteous consciousness and intent.

The more I surrendered the phenomenal world, the more I remembered a mystic lineage. My dark descent into a deep well of love, infinite potentiality, and almost frightening beauty nutrified me like soulful amniotic fluid . . . *Beltane rituals and rites of the moon . . . Imbolc, Lughnasa, Samhain . . . I could hear women beating ancient drums as ancestors came rushing in along with memories of other times. Solstices and equinoxes, cycles, ceremonies, and seasons . . . I walked medicine wheels, evoked cardinal directions, and learned the language of the devas. I lit fires, burned copal, and swam with the Lady of the Lake. I buried treasures in uncharted temples and whispered secrets in the Amazon forest. I danced . .*

Oh, how I danced!

I explored my sexuality in ways that elicited puritanical judgment. I sang prayers, performed holy rites, and spent countless nights writing. I created art using the curves of my body and the seduction of my voice. I gifted my blood to our Mother and healed thousands of bleeding souls. I bowed and bowed deeply, breathing the dirt of an unknown earth. Illumined with inexplicable wonder, I dissolved all that I thought I knew until I touched, suddenly, the untouchable, in one timeless alchemical moment—and everything at once changed.

Every. Single. Thing.

In casting my gaze to the Holy Feminine, in surrendering the very human longing for a familiar frame of feminine reference—the nunnery, white witches, and gathering goddesses—this un-nameable force woke within me. She yawned, and then she stretched into my world, emerging from unmentionable places within. Something cracked open, and a pure luminosity shaped by shadows began to have Her way as my very life.

Absolute abandon. Complete and total release.

Here, now, I could breathe, and breathe deeply. In the immediacy of Her Presence, my exhaustive search ceased to be.

Priestess-in-secret

Riveted and refueling, more questions than answers surfaced like serpents: Who is this She that is waking within me? This informant from another age? This lioness roaring? This most salient of savants? I felt like a tree rooted to the center of the earth and also the mythic condor buoyed by miles of sky. I ached with inexplicable ecstasy, untamed and wild, unwinding from a subterranean nothingness and all-thing-ness of my soul.

My kaleidoscopic let-go was so intimate and sacrosanct and so excruciatingly essential, I dared not risk the scorn of normalcy by naming it. *I was a priestess-in-secret, a hidden acolyte of the feminine face of god, resurrected from moist soil and touched by the sun itself.* Confusing? Yes. Chaotic? Yes. Some moments were wretched and terrifying, while the next were edgeless and timeless.

Had I encountered the Goddess within me? Perhaps. It must've been so. I could certainly feel a rising. *Her* rising. And I knew it couldn't be happening solely in me.

As days turned into months and seasons into years, my sublime communing only begot more questions, most crucial of which was: *Why are so many women still championing our collective victimization in a dying system of toxic masculinity?* The rising of the feminine is not a victimized "me too" movement, for "me too" is actually tipping her hat to the unstoppable surge of the feminine energetic and the waking of the Goddess within us all.

Being that the laboratory of my life is my altar, I tossed out an invitation to a few friends to join my query: What exactly is the feminine energetic? What does that even mean? How does science understand it, and how does it operate? Does it have a particular function? Is it possible to behold? To enhance? To collaborate with?

Our collective excavation began one Sunday in the Larchmont district of Los Angeles, and that Sunday turned into a thousand Sundays of unpacking and dismantling and then remembering and allowing. Before my very eyes, lifting rock after boulder in this venerable excavation, countless courageous women digging deep into the recesses and buried treasures of their souls, an unforeseen invitation revealed over and over again: In order to understand the so-called "goddess within," we'd need to understand, surrender to, and then fully embrace the dynamic and vital sacred masculine.

That's a Big Deal for the half of humanity who has suffered under the oppressive regime of the virulent non-sacred version. And yet, I found no way of getting around it—understanding the encoded masculine became requisite in owning our feminine glory and wonder. For verily, the Holy Feminine births all things, including the potency and power of the masculine.

This is what I was wanting to hear on that bright and sunny day in the cavernous hall of the Beverly Hills Hilton charity luncheon event. That in the vulnerable grace of our surrender to all that we are, we rise embracing, not only the awakening Goddess within us, we rise to acknowledge and understand that each of us carries the catalytic capability and focalized energetics of a consecrated masculine. That when birthed by a luminous feminine resonance, the masculine, which is so much about action and accomplishment, is then able to effect miracles in the blink of an eye.

Dance of the divine

Divine feminine and divine masculine—a resplendent dance of complementary dynamics . . . a divine dance of the cosmos crystallized in the here and now. She is the Life Force itself, and He accentuates her blinding radiance into lucid form. It's all about energetics. You can't have one without the other.

I suspect this is what His Holiness the Dalai Lama means when he says, "The world will be saved by the western woman." He's seen a caliber of woman unfurl her wings on the thermals of the women's movement while witnessing a transcendent feminine awaken and stand as never before. With her endowment of the mighty goddess within, she's able to birth, nurture, *and* get shit done thanks to her heartily developed masculine. And she's able to get it done well.

It's my sneaking suspicion that what the Dalai Lama predicted has more to do with the rising tide of an enlivened feminine energetic than a specified gender. I've found in my own being and in ones I've been honored to serve that this vein of gold His Holiness is intimating has everything to do with a healthy, embodied, and reverential Feminine that lives within us all.

Finding the "goddess within" isn't simply an airy-fairy invitation (or excuse) for women to explore all things femmé via tantalizing talismans and accompanying accouterments available at the local crystal shoppe. Locating, and then allowing the "goddess within" is a necessary step in the evolution of humanity, without vilifying or sacrificing the potency of the magnificent masculine within.

This is the walk of the contemporary priestess, and even—dare I say—the contemporary priest who's not limited by the decaying manacles of a dying patriarchy dedicated to aggression, ownership, dogmatic hierarchy and division.

This is where science meets devotion, where the feminine meets the masculine. If we're truly interested in serving an emerging paradigm of right-relating, the feminine energetic is a wave that must rise. Oriented not in opposition, but compelled by inspired service and limitless contribution. The holy feminine collaborating with the focused functionality of a reverent and noble masculine will deliver new realities.

I believe this to be the true anthem of the modern day feminist— one who understands that it's not enough for us to fight the good fight while championing ideologies and change. I'm certain the only choice we have at this point is to intimately acknowledge the complexity of the human experience while magnifying, uplifting, and even adoring, the feminine resonance within all. Not as victim, not as an object, not on a pedestal, and not as a martyr. In remembering that it is through Her that all of existence is birthed and with right use of the virtuous masculine, we can compose an opus of the ages.

Kate Rodger, PhD is founder and director of the modern day mystery school, Institute of Modern Wisdom, a 501c3 educational foundation. Since 1999, Kate studied under the tutelage of Dr. Michael Bernard Beckwith of Agape International Center, where she is an ordained minister. Having studied with numerous indigenous Elders and Mystics from Africa to the Amazon, and the Far East to home in North America, she's been facilitating trainings-in-consciousness and leading worldwide Mystic Journeys since 2002. In 2006 Kate established the Modern Day Priestess® Trainings, a rigorous ten-moon program which draws from the ancient lineage of Priestess and incorporates New Thought/Ageless Wisdom consciousness to support and empower the walk of the contemporary Priestess that is at once practical and mystic. In 2010, she created the Modern Day Alchemist® Training, the men's counterpart to the MDP training. In 2014, she established the Ojai Love Center located in the Chumash valley of Ojai, CA. In May of 2019, Kate earned her doctoral degree in metaphysics, with a concentration on integral theory and energy medicine. In every aspect of her work, she is deeply committed to Right Relationship, beginning with the self, and extending to All Our Relations. She currently lives in California with her partner. For more information: www.instituteofmodernwisdom.com

Chapter 15

For me, the phrase "You are the source of your own experience" has become a truth hidden in plain sight. A map for an on-going journey of learning, this phrase has had the greatest impact on my understanding of life and what causes us to be happy, successful and fulfilled. And yet the huge focus upon and commercialization of the Law of Attraction has reduced this dynamic down to, "With a bit of positive thinking you will magically manifest the world of your dreams." Unfortunately, this oversimplification means that when things don't go well, it's all too easy to fall into a blaming victim posture, becoming quickly disillusioned with the initial sense of possibility offered by this statement.

Julie Starr

You Are the Source of Your Experience

I was a seeker of truth way before I heard this phrase. Throughout childhood, my sense of needing to understand life was all pervasive: questions such as, what makes us happy? or what does true success look and feel like? were like riddles whispered with urgent longing. Eventually these questions no longer lurked, but instead loomed large, like a teacher at the front of the school room, awaiting my answer. Since ever I'd begun to read or study popular self-help, philosophy or success thinking, I'd been supposedly agreeing with the premise that we are the source of our own experience. The somewhat magical idea that life works from the inside out. I even wrote a novel for young adults on that very topic. I expounded it, I coached others in it. But in the classic difference between knowledge and wisdom, I didn't truly live from it.

Instead, like so many of us on a committed path of enquiry, personal development or spiritual self-discovery, I existed on the surface of my belief for far too long. So while I argued with others for the truth of it, I didn't notice where I was living from an opposing belief, e.g. that I was a victim to haphazard circumstances. I had no idea that beneath my theoretical agreement lurked a structure of sabotaging beliefs I'd adopted early on—beliefs such as life's not fair, success is hard-earned, and fortune favours only the 'special' people. I simply wasn't aware I thought this.

There's another wonderful irony that for so many years, although I supposedly believed that I was the source of everything, I actually wanted to find someone else to tell me the answers. I thought that I should be schooled in some way, e.g. attend a training course, self-development program, read books, etc. So, for at least 35 years I

140

absorbed vast quantities of self-help/self-development material, generally hoping for my own *Eureka!* moment.

We adopt beliefs unknowingly

While I sought the answers I needed, the river of life meandered along, often enjoyably, sometimes uncomfortably, and with twists and turns I seemed unable to control—like not getting my perfect job, relationship, house or that lucky break I'd hoped for. It was as if there were some invisible universal design for my life and my job was to try and negotiate with that. Over time I developed a feeling of being a subtle victim to fate, or karma, in a life less than fair.

For example, I left school at sixteen, which I soon decided set me behind people with more extensive qualifications. As I looked around me, life appeared to favor the gorgeous, talented, well-connected people—which didn't feel like me. My family wasn't rich, or influential in any great way, which I figured was bound to be a further disadvantage. Having invented this illusory barrier, I then needed to create a plan to overcome it. I decided I would need to work really hard to overcome these challenges, and this sense of struggle was what life had intended for me. I accepted this without question. After all, life's not fair is it?

I forged a traditional career for a while, switching jobs, moving towns, trading a feeling of belonging for a better job title, more money, or simply a sense of forward motion. Plus, of course I, read books, attended courses and sustained my personal quest to figure this 'life' thing out. I exercised regularly, avoided TV, and tried to meditate (which I'll admit didn't come easy). I also got married, and whilst I was super-happy to do that, compromise to my life goals became my constant companion.

At some point, the combination of life, enquiry and reflection began to bear fruit. I realized that instead of being governed solely by my head, I also needed to listen to my heart. Also, to stop looking at what others were doing in the name of success and define my own version. I found that what I really loved was supporting others through one-to-one work, and gradually formed my coaching business. Unfortunately, still operating from my backdrop of 'I began behind' box of beliefs, I then went up a gear, working longer hours, travelling, and resting only on vacations. These vacations became more lavish—expensive itineraries designed to compensate for working oh so hard up until that point. And in the classic victim/martyr pose, I often took my laptop.

Life teaches

The wonderful thing about life is that we can trust it to keep showing us where we need to look, until what must be seen is finally made visible. Which in my case means that eventually my work successes no longer fulfilled me, my marriage faltered then failed, and my health fell properly apart. Which as a punch line meant I separated and divorced, was instructed to take a debilitating diagnosis of Lyme disease seriously and stopped work for almost a year. Boom. There it was: the difference between knowledge and wisdom—another universal irony—my life falling apart was the most magical blessing that could have been bestowed on me. Because when much of the fabric of my life was swept away, I needed to focus on what was left, which in my case was the skeleton frame of sabotaging beliefs, values and perspectives that had been holding it all together.

After the building blocks of work, relationship, and health shifted, I realised that my issues followed a pattern that was so familiar that I didn't question their need to be there. And when I began to question them, I saw that until I stopped playing the role of 'victim to life's twists and turns,' then I was always going to feel a little hard done to, or dealt an unfair hand.

I went into 'poor me' for a while, which is only briefly enjoyable, before turning tedious and cloying. Quite quickly I got sick of my own 'what's gone wrong' story, and basically stopped telling it. As I relinquished the victim role, I could really see how I was also the script writer, casting agent and director of everything good, bad and boring that had ever happened. For me that was a priceless realization, which initially sucked and then became the gateway to a future I now feel genuinely excited about.

It took a few years to regain my health, relocate and rebuild my relationships, find my creativity in work and writing again, and actually, that's still on-going. I'm certainly a work in progress and the task is a fun one. What's wonderful about that is, as I cast back over all that's happened, I'm smiling.

Truths are often deceptively simple

When I reflect on what I've learned so far, as in, priceless facts and knowledge, it's probably not enough to fill a small day pack. In fact, what I've *unlearned,* was just as important as what I learned. What I let go of, was often more important than what I acquired. God clearly has a great understanding of irony, because it turns out that I did have all my answers, all along. To de-mystify the potentially mysterious, here's some examples of what I mean:

No.	Unlearned	Learned
1.	You need a good education to succeed/prosper in life.	Life will show you everything you need to know.

2.	The world is a competitive place and so you must be able to compete.	When I look for my own path, follow my own breadcrumbs, life unfolds joyfully.
3.	To achieve anything worthwhile/valuable, I must work incredibly hard (pay a high price).	When I am clear in my focus, and tune to my own sense of right action, things flow more easily.
4.	Real talent is given only to people who are special in some way.	We all have talents and the key to unlocking them is to follow what makes us happy/joyful.
5.	I need to spot what can go wrong, plan ahead and assert control in situations.	Things are always working out for me. I can trust myself and I can trust life.

Turns out it was all in my mind

'Nothing in the world can bother you as much as your own mind, I tell you. In fact, others seem to be bothering you, but it is not other, it is your own mind.' **Sri Sri Ravi Shankar**

By now I've gained a gentler perspective on day-to-day events, which satisfies my overworked/overwhelmed mind. For me, the secret to happiness surfaces from an on-going ability to soothe, quieten and re-focus the mind. By refocussing, I mean that we develop a constant perspective on thoughts and ideas that enable us to experience a sense of well-being, perhaps happiness and even joy. Those enabling thoughts might include:

❖ That everything is as it should be
❖ That I can always choose a more positive, healthy perspective on any situation (and feel better about it for doing so)

144

❖ That things are always working out for me, even when I don't see how

In the past, my focus had become constantly on what I needed to change on the outside, rather than enquiring on the disconnects within. For example:

❖ If my colleague/family member was more like I want them to be, I'd be happy
❖ If my perfect partner would arrive, I'd be happy
❖ If only my partner would change (their behaviour, attitude or beliefs) I'd be happy
❖ If I were given a major publishing/film/record deal, I'd be happy
❖ If I were slimmer/fitter/better looking/wealthier, I'd be happy

What I didn't realise was that to have any of the above beliefs, I first needed to ignore the truth that I am the source of my own experience.

Loving yourself means looking after yourself

This whole 'self-care' concept was something I struggled with, that was until I realized that this whole notion wasn't a romantic ideal, it was something totally practical, realistic and necessary. A bit like they tell you on the airplane - put your own oxygen mask on before trying to help someone else. It's more than a nice idea; in my chosen profession of coaching, basically you don't function for long if you don't look after yourself. As a nuts example, I would often delay going for a pee when I needed to, instead I'd keep working, talking, or just wait until everyone else's needs were met. Eating, sleeping and relaxing/recuperating were also put second to the goal of 'getting everything done' or 'pleasing others.'

Life lesson learned; I now have daily practices designed to soothe my often overworked, and occasionally overwhelmed, mind, to keep it on its own version of the straight and narrow. For example:

1. I eat well/healthily and avoid alcohol – 7/8ths of the time
2. I make sleep important, e.g. hours, quality, my sleep room is a restful haven of calm
3. I meditate daily (mornings are best 15-20 min is average)
4. I listen to heathy stuff, e.g. positive speakers, guided visualisations (I'm a fan of Insights Timer App)
5. I practice yoga regularly, (my vacations often have health/yoga elements to them)
6. I write reflection notes, or 'mind dump,' to clear confusion or troubled thoughts
7. I attend personal development programmes – only stuff I'm genuinely interested in though
8. I stay away from difficult/vexatious people as much as possible, (and instead gravitate towards people I find uplifting)
9. I hardly read or engage in the news
10. I avoid watching TV that's inherently 'down,' fearful or violent in its topics

From a surer inner sense of self arises personal practice

What's been amazingly brilliant is that through all my wanderings, musings and studies, I reckon I've learned how to make myself happy in the everyday. (Which is the appropriate location surely?) The bonus for me is that it's pretty simple, as simple things make me happy. The art is in learning to appreciate them. For example, I can easily appreciate:

❖ A decent cup of English tea
❖ Laughing with friends, dumb jokes, childish humour
❖ A fabulous movie, or piece of creative art

- ❖ Clean sheets, comfy bedding and turning out the light with the knowledge of getting a good night's rest
- ❖ A walk in the woods with a friend, dogs off their leads, nonsense chat, out in nature
- ❖ Wearing certain clothes— soft fabrics, fabulous designs, or simply casual comfort
- ❖ Sunshine, blue sky, natural warmth my body can relax with

I promise you, this list is a monster retail park away from what I used to think I needed to make me happy!

Learning without end

By now, I see that life has masses more to offer me, and my learning is in my every day. I'm alright with that, I appreciate all of it, and I welcome whatever is coming. I combine positive intentions with a sense of personal responsibility and things tend to work out pretty well, pretty much all of the time. If something isn't as I want it, I'm much quicker to ask, 'what is my part in creating this?' I do still find myself wanting to blame others/life for things that show up that I don't want, but ultimately, I know that's useless nonsense bound to end up nowhere I'm interested in.

Oh, and if I need the restroom? Yeah, don't even bother, I'm already gone.

Julie Starr is an expert and thought leader in the field of coaching and mentoring. Since 2002, her best-selling book *The Coaching Manual* has supported the evolution of the coaching field through simple, powerful ideas and practical approaches. Her books are translated into many languages and are required reading on coach training programs around the world. With over 20 years and thousands of hours coaching experience, Julie works with executives from some of the world's largest organizations. Julie supports powerful people to align to their ultimate potential for joy and contribution. Her approach is challenging, compassionate and empowers clear leadership. Julie's books, *Brilliant Coaching* and *The Mentoring Manual* support managers and leaders to improve business performance by developing people. She lectures in universities and at industry conferences to inspire understanding and engagement. Julie is MD of Starr Coaching, a leading provider of coach training in organizations, check out www.starrcoaching.co.uk. Julie also writes novels for young adults and donates proceeds to charities which house, heal and educate street children and orphans; check out www.ruffdogbooks.com

Chapter 16

I chose "Enlightenment is something you can attain" because in my many years of reading and listening to the regurgitated wisdom of ancient sages and attending workshops, I found it frustrating to discover that *only if* I was disciplined and mindful enough and persevered long enough with a specific ritual at a specific time of the day, I *might* attain a state of consciousness that would silence my mind, allow me to see and feel everything as connected, and achieve my infinite potential. Linking enlightenment to any requirement that involves the repeating of complex efforts and rituals to attain infinite potential is gravely misleading and yet spiritual seekers are still being lead down this path. Watering it down to make it seem like a cool spiritual goal to attain takes one far from realizing our inherent and enlightened nature.

Linda Sechrist

Enlightenment Is Something You Can Attain—Not!

Human beings are the only species on the planet that strive to achieve something more than we think we are. Personally I thought enlightenment would be the answer to all my ills and prayers, and it became an all-consuming goal I sought to attain.

For 42 years I had intellectualized and analyzed life in my head, suffering from high levels of anxiety and panic attacks. When the anxiety got too bad, I split and lived outside myself, disconnected from my body and my feelings. My mind never shut up. It played continual loop re-runs of conversations I'd had as well as rehearsed conversations that I rarely mustered up the courage to have.

Then I entered the spiritual arena, and the enlightenment and the seeking game was on.

Desperately trying to heal a dysfunctional childhood, adolescence and early adulthood, I gained lots of spiritual striving experience between 1989 and 2004, turning to psychotherapy and personal development courses. I invested substantial sums of money and time in workshops and online summits as well as in hundreds of books that mostly delivered pithy wisdom on how fasting, journaling, affirmations, intentions, guided meditation, breathing, mandalas, ceremony, and chanting might unlock quantum powers that would transform my mind from a storm of critical chatter into a serene sea of peace and help me achieve a state of enlightened bliss.

I lived a high-wire act of swinging from no self-esteem to low self-esteem without a safety net of self-identity. Overcoming the issue of enmeshment was especially daunting, as I experienced myself as an extension of my mother, with no sense of where she stopped and I began. It's why my therapist had to explain to me what she meant by 'you have no boundaries.' Thanks to an excellent therapist, the late John Bradshaw who championed inner child work in his books, which I devoured, and author Melanie Beatty who awakened me to my co-dependent behavior, the Adult Children of Alcoholics program and *A Course in Miracles*, I began to sense that a sense of personal integrity and wholeness was possible. In retrospect this part of my healing process is something that I call a spiritual striptease. One-by-one the veils that kept the real Self hidden had to be removed.

I am fortunate that I also learned and eventually accepted from all of my reading, spiritual teachers, and satsang's at the feet of enlightened masters such as Yogi Amrit Desai and Mooji, that being enlightened or awake is not something that any one of us can achieve, attain, or become because *this is what we already are*. My two-pound brain, home to the ego's collection of misguided self-images and defense mechanisms, can never do more than struggle to intellectually understand this. But I could feel my heart resonating with this Truth, and slowly I ceased striving to become enlightened and settled into a slow and sporadic pace of awakening, accepting that it would come.

A natural evolution

Although I no longer pursue enlightenment, thousands of individuals continue striving to achieve this impossible spiritually-mandated goal that arose after the Western world first learned of enlightenment from the media frenzy surrounding the trip The Beatles made to India to meet the Maharishi Mahesh Yogi, who introduced the West to Transcendental Meditation.

My journey to cease striving for the unattainable began with the realization that the "what" I needed to do in spiritual terms was to negate that which I am not—body, mind, and personhood—life's biggest accoutrements. The "how" to do it was made clear by dozens of spiritual sources: turn inward and "know myself" through self-inquiry utilizing two questions, "Who am I?" and "Why am I here?"

Both questions are geared to bring about epiphanies such as enlightenment and have nothing to do with knowledge and learning and everything to do with *unlearning*, shedding false self-images and beliefs I'd acquired from my home, school, and religious environments as well as my culture. Negation, which I learned from Krishnamurti's teaching, was the perfect tool for shedding my false self-images. It immediately began to slowly diminish their existence without striving or struggling, which would only concretize the very thing I thought I was.

I've had plenty to negate while I've waited for "no me" to show itself!

Thankfully I've also had help from the many mentors that I found in books and from our magical eavesdropping Universe. The earliest awakening seeds that were planted came in the form of other questions I heard my earliest teacher, J. Krishnamurti, ask in his 1974 *Art of Living* dialogues with Alan W. Anderson, Emeritus Professor of Religious Studies at San Diego State University. One particular question, "Is it possible for the mind to empty itself of its contents?" haunted me, even in my dreams. The question begged an answer, which I found some hint of when I discovered that any time I was fully present to what I was doing (not thinking about what I was doing but rather just doing), or when there was real closure to something rather than leaving parts of it dangling and unfinished, my mind was not on "record." Which meant there would be no content for the mind to empty. Truth, Krishnamurti taught me, is a pathless land and freedom from all that I knew of any belief system.

The seeds of this slower, non-striving, "let life happen" approach to self-realization began to produce little green shoots not long after I stumbled into the world of immersive journalism in 2004, writing for the publication that would become *Natural Awakenings*. Although I've not been allowed to write for its four million readers in a first-person format, I have been an attentive witness to my exploration and experimentation into the subjects that I write about—healthy lifestyles, the mind/body connection, spirituality and the science of consciousness.

It's embarrassing to admit that until I did a recent archeological dig through a box of my early articles, I hadn't recognized the extent to which Grace has influenced my life and provided the perfect tool for my unfoldment. No need for striving on my part! I went from writing an occasional article in what in 1995 was a free bi-monthly, 16-page *Awakenings* newsletter, to writing for a 40-page Southwest Florida resource magazine for personal and planetary health. The evolution of the publication, which began in Ohio in 1993 and in 2004 caught fire in Southwest Florida, is worth noting because of the synchronicities involved.

The original *Awakenings* newsletter was hand-copied on a Xerox machine, hand-stapled and distributed to alert people to classes at The Center of Balance, a New Age bookstore in Courtland, Ohio. It closed when the owner died. But *Natural Awakenings* grew into a franchise publication with 70-plus publishers located throughout the US. In a nutshell, the choice of right livelihood that I first learned about at age 46 from Krishnamurti's *Art of Living* video series, which I saw at The Center of Balance, is what unconsciously guided me in 2004 onto the perfect path for my maturation and individuation.

Only after reflection did I recognize that my first national writing assignment for *Natural Awakenings* was a window with a preview of what was to come over the next 15 years. My interview with Angaangaq Angakkorsuaq, fondly known as "Uncle," introduced me to the world of shamanism. A healer, storyteller and carrier of the Qilaut (windrum), the Eskimo-Kalaallit Elder from Greenland was traveling to Florida to present his "Melting the Ice in the Heart of Man" workshop. Near the end of our interview he invited me to attend. We still communicate occasionally via Facebook while he globetrots and speaks from the heart to wake people up to the perils of climate change. I help his cause with my articles on the environment and my volunteer work as a core member of a local chapter of the Pachamama Alliance, which works internationally to create an environmentally sustainable, spiritually-fulfilling, socially-just human presence on our planet—a New Dream for humanity.

Since my telephone interview with Uncle, I've had numerous epiphanies, received occasional audible messages from a disembodied voice and studied Integrative Amrit yoga and yoga nidra with two of the world's renowned teachers, Yogi Amrit Desai and Yogeshwari Kamini Desai. "Choose to live deliberately," didn't seem like a really profound epiphany at the time, but it took me 20-plus years to get the deeper meaning and what I was being directed to do—live life every day acknowledging that I am energy enlivened by the same intelligence that runs the Universe and that I am not the doer of the actions.

My work with *Natural Awakenings* has blessed me with the opportunity to do hundreds of telephone interviews with ordinary people doing extraordinary work that makes them the change they want to see in the world. Additionally, I've been blessed to have precious, uninterrupted one-on-one telephone conversations with luminaries such as Dr. Bruce Lipton, Gregg Braden, Dr. Wayne Dyer, Dr. Jean Houston, Dr. Jean Shinoda Bolen, Apollo 14 Astronaut Edgar Mitchell, John Hagelin, Cate Montana, Dr. Jill Bolte Taylor, Seijaku Roshi, Laurie McCammon, Dr. Ron Dalrymple, Raymond Moody, and Dr. Eben Alexander, as well as remarkable energy healers such as Donna Eden and Gary Sinclair. Each of these, as well as others too numerous to name, elicited insights that continue shifting aspects of the paradigm I live in.

Reading books by the authors I interviewed, sent to me beforehand by publishing houses, and interviewing as well as writing articles, cultivated, fertilized and helped to raise my inner garden of consciousness. I was continually affirmed in my belief that not only do I live in the Universe, the Universe lives in me. Such intuitions weakened my sense of personhood, strengthened my sense of cosmic identity and affirmed that those of us who feel we are here on Earth to serve during these times of chaos, are answering the call of conscious evolution. I am, as you are, receiving an evolutionary call to become a conscious explorer creating new ways of being together in communities and to help create a new story that serves the common good of everyone. There has never been another time on this planet when recognizing this call has been more important.

Inevitable return

The last time the "I" almost disappeared was in 1991 when my only child left home to backpack through Europe, my seven-year love relationship ended, and the company I worked for was hard hit by an economic downturn. They downsized. I lost my job. I was no one's mother, no one's wife or lover, and no one's employee. I wasn't even anyone's daughter, sister or aunt because I had no family in the area— they were 12 hours away. With no one or any thing to identify with, I fought to stay awake at night because I was afraid that if I fell asleep I would disappear.

Several years ago, when the I began to disappear again, there was no fear or anxiety. Simply the acknowledgment of the no-thing that can't be attained or achieved.

What I've come to know for certain is that I could never sense this evolutionary call unless I am an integral aspect of what is calling me. When I first turned inward, I was longing for wholeness and got my first remembering of that state when I read the lines of Biblical scripture in Jeremiah 1:5, "I knew you before I formed you in your mother's womb." That one sentence spoken by God to the prophet Jeremiah evoked a knowing within me that resonated in my bones. The reason I felt longing was because before I manifested as life in this body, I was wholly complete within the Cosmic Intelligence that runs the Universe and operates my body.

Think about it. If you taste a recipe that needs salt, you know this because you've tasted it before when it was salted.

Unlike others who have glory halleluiah instantaneous awakenings, mine has been the slow erosion of beliefs veiling the fact that I am awake as Being. As a late bloomer, I was delighted when Dr. Ron Dalrymple, the producer of *The Endless Question,* a "shockumentary" on consciousness, asked me to be in his film—a film that includes a profound Nikola Tesla quote, "Once we begin to investigate the energy aspects of who we are as human beings, it will change everything."

Tesla's quote brought back an old memory of what had initially sparked my spiritual quest and changed my life more than 30 years ago. It was Barbara Brennan's *Hands of Light,* the first book I ever read on the human energy field and how the body can heal itself if it is given everything it needs. The memory morphed into an OMG! moment when I recalled a different quote by T. S. Elliot, "We shall not cease from exploration, and the end of all our exploring will be to arrive where we started and know the place for the first time."

I was back at the beginning of my exploration and knew the Self for the first time. I also knew that the cliché "what we dwell upon we become" is true. Although I had taken up various spiritual practices and never stuck with them, I really didn't need them. My work has been my spiritual practice for 15 years. Like the bud of a rose, I've unfolded and the lines have blurred between my inner and outer life. It appears that the evolution from me to "no me" is naturally inevitable when I am open, curious, vulnerable, and oh so willing to let go of all of my history that I can pour my heart into a prayer I learned from Mooji—"All the concepts and images of myself, I lay at your feet. Absorb me in you—and realize that there is no enlightenment of I, me and myself as a person. Rather it is in dropping these veils that the Self awakens to its mistaken identity as a person. No effort can bring about such a transformation."

Linda Sechrist is the *Natural Awakenings* Senior Staff Writer, Director of Community Outreach, New Franchise Managing Editor and a member of the healthy lifestyle magazine's national editorial team. Her writing career has provided a rare opportunity to align purpose and passion in educating nearly four million readers on Awareness, the environment, and wellness. Graced with an avocation where her gifts and talents are used for the good of all, Linda has organized and hosted Rethinking Health Matters, an online radio show, as well as the first online Metabolic Revolution Syndrome summit. A trained facilitator for Integrated Amrit Yoga Nidra, Linda is a bestselling author published in the Inspired Living e-books *Wisdom of MidLife Women2* and *Unleash Your Inner Magnificence*. She joined author Laurie McCammon and other women in co-authoring the *Enough! How to Liberate Yourself and Remake the World with Just One Word Guidebook*. Linda has been telling meaningful stories of change agents for 25 years. From vast research and thousands of interviews, she is certain that change is the only currency, that there is not one answer to any problem, that no one knows everything, and that consciousness is nudging each of us to awaken and come together now. For more information: LindaSechrist.com

Chapter 17

Conscious leadership is a by-product of the mindfulness movement, and conscious leaders, at their best, are trained to focus on the "we" rather than the "me" in any given circumstance, bringing their highest level of awareness to that situation. Unlike conscious business or even conscious media, there is no official process and little transparency to verify the authenticity of a person's claim of being a conscious leader. Unfortunately, conscious leadership has become a buzzword with some very unconscious people claiming that title for marketing purposes. It's like people believe that being spiritually oriented automatically makes them a conscious leader, resulting in a great deal of confusion, disillusionment and bitterness in company environments, diluting its meaningfulness.

TRINA WYATT

GETTING CONSCIOUS ABOUT CONSCIOUS LEADERSHIP

Conscious leadership is a relatively new term, a new concept, born out of the rising interest in consciousness, meditation, neuroscience and spirituality. Leadership, whether conscious or unconscious, has everything to do with how people are guided in working as a group towards a common goal. In conscious leadership, leaders of that group are supposed to have a level of awareness and caring of how their choices and behaviors impact that group, the company's vision, and the world at large.

For the first half of my life, I thought leadership was either bestowed from those with more power or it was a popularity game based upon superficial qualities such as charisma and glib speech. There also seemed to be a consensus that with leadership the ends justify the means. As long as you accomplished the goal and people acquiesced, who cared about how you got there?

During the second half of my life, I realized that the ends do not justify the means, that leadership is bestowed by those being led, not self-proclaimed or bestowed by the most powerful (as in a dictatorship), and that to be successful and effective both leaders and those being led need to have a certain level of consciousness and self-love.

Baptism by fire

I was first called to lead in the third grade. My teacher, Mrs. Kobayashi, encouraged me to run for our class's student council representative, which consisted of standing in front of the class and showing them samples of our hand-writing. I was a bit shocked when I won by a landslide. (The final vote was something like 30 to 7.) I had no idea why I was chosen. I remember feeling proud but also a bit of a fraud. Was being good at penmanship the equivalent to being a good leader?

By the time I was eleven, my goal in life was to work in the film business. I loved movies. I loved how they could make you feel and how they showed different ways of living and being in the world. But bowing to my father's "job security" based career advice, I went to UCLA, majored in economics, minored in accounting and, upon graduation, immediately went to work at one of the "Big Six" accounting firms. But I didn't give up on my dream of working in the film business. I scoured the newspaper want ads and responded to an ad for Assistant Controller for, "the largest independent film company in Hollywood," Carolco Pictures. When I got the job and an unexpected increase in salary *after* I accepted the offer but *before* I started working, I should have known something was up.

Unbeknownst to me, the company had laid off half of their employees the day before I started. Needless to say, the remaining employees weren't too friendly. Then two weeks later the Controller who hired me gave his notice. At age 24, with less than a month's experience, I went from having no supervisory experience to inexplicably leading the finance team, hoping no one would call me out as a fraud. I stayed at Carolco and worked as the Assistant Controller, continuing to manage the accounting department for two and a half years.

Out of this baptism by fire I learned the following: 1) Even if you don't feel like a leader and don't know exactly what you're doing, just act as if you do until reality catches up; 2) Most people want to be told what to do and not think for themselves; 3) Treat others as you would like to be treated; 4) If you are too nice you risk losing respect and therefore your effectiveness; 5) Say what you are going to do and then do it and finally; 6) Instilling fear of job security is a powerful way to get people to obey, but it doesn't instill respect or create a pleasant work environment.

At this point I still hadn't learned the importance of self-love. I was in a profession I disliked (accounting) in order to please my father. I had little self-respect, telling myself that I only had the job because no one else wanted it and that my employees listened to me because they didn't think they could get another job that paid as well.

It wasn't until many years later that my belief in my abilities to lead were established and I learned one of the major keys to conscious leadership: Taking the focus off of myself and focusing on other people. I had worked as the COO of Tribeca Entertainment since 1996, managing the office rental business, the Tribeca Film Center, and the finance and operations of the production business, basically steering the ship so that my boss Jane, Robert De Niro's partner, could focus on producing movies. Then, in early 2001, she asked me how we should go about building the Tribeca brand.

"Start a film festival," I said.

"OK," Jane replied. "I'll set up a meeting with Bob for you to come in and pitch the idea."

That meeting went well, and I was given the green-light to move forward in planning the Festival for May of 2002. I was well into planning and then came September 11.

Tribeca was less than a half mile from the World Trade Center, and, like everyone who experienced the attacks first-hand, we were all traumatized. As the most senior executive at the company, I became a counselor and a shoulder for everyone in the company and in the Film Center to lean on. We needed to grieve and we needed to heal, and we all consciously worked together to build the Festival as a means of bringing the entire community of lower Manhattan together and bring hope back to the struggling economy.

We were working to create something far greater than ourselves and this brought forth love and compassion. I learned then, that when you are working towards something greater than yourself, self-love blossoms and there is no room for self-doubt.

But in launching the first Tribeca Film Festival, I also became painfully aware of the egos in the film business and the low depths that people were willing to sink even in the name of altruism. Why couldn't visual stories be used to help in personal growth and ultimately make the world a better place? Why couldn't this be done with integrity? I was in the midst of starting a regime of self-care, spiritual development, and personal growth, going to therapy to address my shadow, reading inspiring self-help and spiritual books, practicing yoga and meditating. Was it possible to combine my love of all things spiritual and my love of film? I vowed that if I couldn't work in film on these terms I would no longer work in the industry.

And yet from 2003 until 2013, I didn't step into my dream. My excuse was financial. I needed a job that could pay for a family of four to live comfortably in Los Angeles. So I fell back into finance work and became the CFO for a large animation film production company. Once again, I was miserable, falling into a mid-life crisis, buying a Porsche, flirting with an extra-marital affair, and shopping for things I didn't need for distraction. Fortunately, I hit rock-bottom and got up the courage to tell my husband I was quitting my job as CFO and would never again work for just a paycheck. Bless him, he agreed, and several months later we were living in a smaller house in Boulder, Colorado, where I assumed the role of Chief Content Officer for the largest streaming platform dedicated to transformational entertainment in the US.

Not-so-conscious media

Conscious media tells stories that inspire connection to oneself, to others and to something greater. Conscious media supports an awareness that individual choices have a ripple effect throughout the world, that ultimately we are all the same and that our individual consciousness is part of a greater consciousness.

And yet, working full-time in the consciousness arena, I have been shocked at the lack of consciousness. The number of people proudly calling themselves "conscious leaders" who still haven't mastered their egos, or frankly even tried, are legion. Spiritual righteousness is the most common pitfall to which every aspirant on the spiritual path falls prey, what Buddhist teacher Trungpa Rinpoche describes as seeing spirituality as a process of *self-improvement*—the impulse to develop and refine the ego when the ego is, by nature, essentially empty.

"The problem is that ego can convert anything to its own use," he says, "even spirituality." People afflicted with spiritual righteousness have inflated egos because they believe that they have been working on themselves, following a path of study and practice, and therefore see themselves as superior to others who they perceive have done less or studied differently. There is a self-righteousness in their practice. They think "my way is the only way," and have a "let me tell you what you need to do and who you need to be" approach to relationship.

Being right and self- righteous, making others wrong, and using fear as motivation are the old hallmarks of "leaders" in industry. I had believed the consciousness arena and what's called "conscious capitalism" would not be prone to all of this. I was wrong.

Several years ago, I was on the C-level team of one particular media company that outwardly led in conscious media. Inwardly it was a whole different story. I don't think I have ever worked in a more fear-based culture. It was devastating to witness leaders trapped in the self-righteous leadership role who ended-up abusing others and themselves, wasting so much promise and potential, clearly showing how to NOT be a conscious leader.

For example, I was in a company-wide executive level meeting and one of the most senior executives proceeded to publicly dress-down another executive, saying, "That's the stupidest idea I've ever heard." Another time, running my first content meeting to which he was invited, he told me, "That was the worst meeting agenda I've ever seen." He didn't pull either of us aside and privately say these things in a way to help us improve upon our performance. No, he said it in front of our colleagues to demean and criticize us and to reinforce his superiority. When I finally spoke to him about his behavior and how it reinforced a fear-based corporate culture, it was as if he had never heard of the polarities of fear and love.

Another colleague at this conscious media company prioritized looking good and posturing in order to dominate and further her personal agenda. She subtly undermined colleagues in many ways, primarily by coming late to meetings or not attending at all, avoiding any confrontation, and talking behind the peoples' backs as a means to try to change a situation.

But how could I or anyone else expect anything more? The culture, climate and practices of any company are set by the CEO. The CEO of this same company let fear lead primarily by controlling situations by withholding information and not putting decisions or directives in writing, so that they could later be retracted or denied. He not only practiced win-lose negotiations, but prided himself on winning at the expense of others losing big. Though he supposedly had multi-millions, he lived and practiced in a constant state of lack. Under his "leadership," business practices were to nickel and dime our suppliers, prioritizing short-term results over long-term relationships.

Ego fuels scarcity and considers life, especially business, to be a zero-sum game. Ultimately it was the fear-based culture and my team's unwillingness to see the culture for what it was and its impact on the employees and the success of the company's vision that triggered my departure.

Conscious leadership defined

So how would I define conscious leadership? First off, consciousness is more than mindfulness or a meditation practice. Being conscious means being aware at multiple levels. It means the mind is aware of being aware. In business being conscious means taking all stake-holders into consideration, including the public and the environment. It means using business as a force for good and for advancing humanity and global wellbeing. It also means a company should exist for a higher purpose than simply making money.

At its core, conscious leadership is leading as a spiritual practice for the leader and possibly, for those being led. Richard Griffiths, Founder of the 3Q Institute, says, "Spiritual intelligence is a higher dimension of intelligence that activates the qualities and capabilities of the authentic self (or the soul) in the form of wisdom, compassion, integrity . . . and love."

Both the commitment to personal growth and a spiritual practice require a willingness to be uncomfortable. Both a leader and those being led need to be vulnerable enough to be able to give and receive constructive feedback. "True love" is supporting the growth of another without resorting to fear. As my teacher Yogi Bhajan says, "Kindness, compassion, and caring with love is real love. That doesn't mean you can't tell someone they're wrong. If they are wrong and you don't tell them, you are a coward. If you don't confront, you can't elevate."

Conscious leadership is listening, setting an example, walking the talk and role modeling without claiming infallibility. Probably one of the more important qualities of a conscious leader is being able to recognize that you are fallible and learn from your mistakes. According to Arianna Huffington, "We need to accept that we won't always make the right decisions, that we'll screw up royally sometimes . . . understanding that failure is not the opposite of success, it's part of success."

Leading is more than being the "brand" or "the face" on an organization. Conscious leadership is about collaboration, and collaboration is only possible when leaders believe other people also have unique contributions to offer the world. As Benjamin Zander writes in *The Art of Possibility*, "A monumental question for leaders in any organization to consider is: How much greatness are we willing to grant people?"

Conscious leaders also practice gratitude. According to studies, a grateful leader is more likely to be viewed as successful, and when team leaders express gratitude, frequently and specifically, team members are more engaged in their work, more loyal to the organization, work harder and experience greater overall wellbeing.

Though I've been critical of some of my former employers and leaders in the conscious media arena, I am truly grateful for the lessons they have taught me. I couldn't be where I am now without these life experiences.

In summary, being a conscious leader requires humbleness and a level of mastery over the mind and the ego. The only way I have been able to consistently do this is by maintaining a daily meditation and yoga practice, consciously integrating mind-body-spirit, balancing and subjugating them to my authentic self. My meditation practice helps me to question my thoughts and creates a space to choose my response to a situation, instead of acting out of habit or emotion. If I miss a day of practice, it shows in my managing of situations and people. I am much more judgmental, impatient and even short-tempered. But by connecting to my inner-self daily and reinforcing the feeling that I am connected to something greater, I've learned self-love and have been able to extend that love to others.

Finally, after years of a dedicated daily practice and learning by trial and error, I feel authentically able to consciously lead.

Trina Wyatt launched Conscious Good, a community-driven media platform committed to elevating consciousness, because she believes that visual stories have the power to change the world. Conscious Good envisions a world where everyone feels connected to themselves, to each other and to something greater. To fulfill on this vision, Conscious Good created a monthly film series to bring the best in Mind-Body-Spirit Cinema to yoga studios and spiritual centers around the world, as well as the Conscious Good Creators Network, an innovative social network to support visual storytellers and their work. Considered a leader in the conscious media movement, Trina has spoken at numerous national events on the topic of media/entertainment and its impact. One of Trina's most notable career achievements was launching the Tribeca Film Festival for Robert De Niro and taking the reins as its first Festival Director. Trina has also held leadership positions with entertainment companies such as Gaia, Prana Studios, Intrepid Pictures, Withoutabox (sold to Amazon), Film Independent, Turner Pictures and Carolco Pictures. Trina received her MBA from NYU and her BA from UCLA, is a certified Kundalini yoga teacher and was recently honored to join the group, Evolutionary Leaders. She can be reached at: www.ConsciousGood.com

Chapter 18

I have firsthand experience with cancer, and let me tell you I was not leaving my life in the hands of healing white light, vision boards and positive thinking. Yes, I did use alternative healing modalities to help me heal. But the true source of my success in ridding my body of cancer was taking responsibility for my health and approaching healing from every angle of mind, body and spirit. Far too many people in the spiritual community believe you can just sit back, be positive, surround yourself with this imaginary healing white light, create a vision board and magically everything in your body will be healed. Doing this, people never get to the root cause of their disease, condition or symptoms, with the bottom line effect that people remain needlessly sick and can ultimately die.

LISA DIMOND

IT TAKES MORE THAN POSITIVE THOUGHTS

Positivity, healing white light and vision boards can heal the illness in your body. I certainly wish this were true because life, health and wellness would be so easy then! However, maybe just like you, I have experienced life, health, and wellness as a struggle, both personally and professionally.

On January 1, 2013, I woke up early, felt grateful for a new year and declared to myself it was going to be my best year ever. Having just witnessed a very dear friend, a vibrant 87-year-old woman pass away in 17 days, I was reminded that life is short. The year 2013 was going to be the time where I finally did what I wanted to do: get my personal training certification and open a boutique fitness studio. Between grieving for my friend's passing and meeting the world with a new attitude, I forgot about the hardness in my breast that I had noticed just the month prior.

By March 2013, I was on my path with a clear vision for my future and excited about life. Within two months of starting my new business, I went from zero to 23 clients. I loved helping people achieve their health and fitness goals. In March 2013, I celebrated my 48th birthday by going hang gliding, something that had been on my bucket list. In the same month, I made an appointment with my plastic surgeon to have my breast implants checked and get a mammogram. The next available appointment was May.

May 8, 2013 in the late afternoon, I eagerly went to my plastic surgeon appointment. The doctor and I sat in his office and talked. I explained the hardness that I felt in my left breast and that I thought it might be my implant. He agreed that it sounded like an encapsulated implant. When he examined me and felt the hardness, he looked me in the eye and said, "That is not your implant." He turned to the nurse and said, "Order a mammogram and ultrasound. STAT!" I thought to myself, *STAT? Isn't that what doctors say when someone is dying?*

We all know that waiting to do a medical test can take days and even weeks. Not so when the doctor orders a test STAT. My doctor appointment was 3 pm on a Wednesday. My mammogram and ultrasound were scheduled at 8:20 the next morning. Twelve days later I heard the words, "I'm sorry my dear. I don't have good news." That "news" was a late stage, aggressive, rare form of breast cancer—a lobular carcinoma that accounts for just 10 percent of all breast cancer cases. At the time of diagnosis I asked the doctor to not tell me the survival rate. I had a feeling it was low, and it was (36 percent). I was in that room for at least another 30 minutes, though I do not remember another word he said.

The next thing I remember was sitting in my car in the parking lot. I was angry and screaming at the top of my lungs, "Are you fucking kidding me? Why?" over and over again. And then I wondered how I was going to tell the few friends who knew I was at that appointment? And then I sobbed, feeling like I had been sucker punched in the gut! How was I going to tell my two beautiful daughters, ages 15 and 18? My heart broke at the thought.

Living day-to-day

When I was diagnosed, I was completely healthy physically, emotionally and spiritually. I had not been to a doctor in nine years. I hadn't even had a cold. I was physically in the best shape of my life at the age of 48. I had a personal training business and was about to open my own studio. Emotionally, I had never been stronger or more clear, and spiritually I had finally arrived in a loving space.

And then the cancer rollercoaster ride began—doctor appointments, tests, blood work. Here's a snapshot from the month of May 2013: Diagnosis, surgery, brain MRI, chemo, radiation, cancer free, open a business, cancer scare, surgery, infection, shingles, really bad infection, hospital (almost die), chronic fatigue, organ failures, malnourished, elevated tumor markers, probably depressed . . .

Battling cancer became a full time job. If I wasn't at a doctor appointment, a test of some sort, blood work, chemo infusion for five hours, a radiation appointment, I was researching like a fanatic. I was NOT going to be one of their statistics.

Within a few days of being diagnosed, having had time to reflect, feel and analyze the situation, I knew exactly why I had breast cancer. I had been on an emotional rollercoaster practically my entire life. My childhood was no fairy tale, though from an outside perspective it may have looked that way. In stark contrast, behind closed doors, the atmosphere was volatile, full of addiction and shrouded in secrecy. "What happens in this house, stays in this house" was a family rule. This is when I would learn the art of perfectionism. If I was good enough, or better or perfect maybe my mom would feel better. My mother was beautiful, funny and kind on the good days and angry, sad and lonely on the bad days. Early in my childhood I remember there being more good days then bad. But, the first time I ran away from home I was four years old. I packed my Barbie suitcase and called my grandmother to come get me. Without hesitation, she did. She was my lifeline, my superhero.

I remember learning in 8th grade science class that Valium was a drug, not a vitamin. That day, I realized that my mother had an addiction problem, Valium and alcohol. Of course, my father was aware of the situation and I'm certain other family members were as well, but nobody talked about it. My parents relationship was volatile, so much screaming, yelling and throwing things. My father would come home later and later with each passing year until one day he left and never came back. I was 11 years old. I felt abandoned. How could he leave me with her and my two younger brothers? Abandonment issues would plague me for years.

Much later in my life, in my mid-thirties, my mother was finally, officially, diagnosed as bi-polar and schizophrenic. Her struggle was real and my heart still breaks for her, rest her soul. Having been exposed to addiction and high conflict situations on a regular basis in order to cope with the pain and confusion, I unconsciously developed the art of emotional detachment. The truth is, I learned early in my life how to survive in unstable environments. My emotional toolbox was complete: perfectionism, emotional detachment and leave the relationship before someone could leave me.

These unhealthy tools were tested over and over again through my adult life but never as much as in the beginning of 2000 when I lost my father to lung cancer. I was devastated and yet I did not have the skills to express my grief or my sadness. I could not find comfort from family, friends or God. In 2002, still reeling from the loss of my father, my grandmother passed away. From my earliest memories, she had always been the stabilizing force in my life. It was the unconditional love of this woman that kept me believing in myself. And then in 2003, I received a life-shattering phone call that my brother was found dead in his home at the age of 36. His lifelong struggle with addiction had tragically ended. I was angry, full of resentment and grief stricken from the loss of the closest people in my life. But I suppressed these emotions. I buried my thoughts and feelings, put a smile on my face, and kept the facade of my perfect little life with my perfect kids and my perfect job and my perfect marriage.

It wasn't until 2004 that I realized how unhappy I was, how imperfect everything really was. I remember looking in the mirror one day, saying out loud, "I have no idea who you are." I was in my 30s and had completely lost myself. My addiction to perfectionism was taking its toll, and I was physically exhausted. Harboring sadness, grief, guilt, anger and resentment left me emotionally drained. I had no connection to myself, my higher self or a higher power and felt void of spirit and faith. This would also be the year that I left my marriage, packed up my two young daughters and moved to Florida.

My separation and subsequent divorce really spurred me into lots of personal growth. I bought every self-help book I could find and devoured them. I tried traditional therapy, but that didn't work because I wasn't quite ready to discuss the past, my childhood or my marriage. Instead, I began searching for less traditional therapies, looking for a quick fix, the easy path. For six years, I tried it all, psychics, past life regression, tarot card readings, hypnosis, reiki, soul therapy, numerology, healing light therapy, crystal therapy, manifestation seminars, karmic healing, vision boards. I've probably forgotten a few. I searched for anything outside of myself to heal my pain, both physical and emotional, to ease my grief, to settle my anger and to release my resentment.

Then, in August 2010, a friend gifted me a personal growth weekend course. I reluctantly went as a favor to her with no intention of actually participating for my own benefit. I had become disillusioned with personal growth and healing because nothing was working. Much to my surprise, the first three-day course changed my life. It was not a weekend of positive affirmations, sweetness and light. We did intense personal work. We did role playing and acted out things we needed to deal with. I started to figure out what was no longer serving me, and I was able to begin releasing some of the limiting beliefs I had been carrying with me for years.

It was a personal growth experience that took me out of my comfort zone and forced me to deal with my past, take a risk to grow up emotionally, really connect to other human beings and change my ways. I continued with the follow-up courses for years, learning skills that played directly into my cancer recovery.

Doing the work

I can tell you unequivocally that the years of suppressing emotions played a role in my body developing cancer. Our mind, body and spirit are all interconnected and there are plenty of clinical studies that prove it. Unfortunately, this connection has been, to my way of thinking, hugely overplayed by people in the spirituality arena. Yes, the mind affects the body and the emotions affect the body, but healing the body—especially something like cancer—takes more than affirmations, candles and meditation.

When I was diagnosed, I became a research fanatic. I was looking for anything and everything that was going to give me an advantage. And trust me when I say I found *everything* under the sun that promised to cure cancer. At the same time I was deluged with spiritual "advice." I knew people meant well, but you wouldn't believe the things some people suggested. I had one friend in particular who felt that all I needed to do was to create a vision board for my perfect health state and some ancient Native American salve and I could cure myself! I went to healers that taught me how to surround myself in white healing light and healers that assigned me a guardian angel and healers that said I couldn't afford the luxury of a negative thought, and they all assured me that I would be "okay." Seriously?

Sure, I had a "no negativity" policy, but there were some days that just plain sucked. You can remain positive, but on the days when you feel angry, sad or lonely or scared, which is totally normal, it's important to express those emotions. It is far worse to hold them in for the sake of positivity.

Bottom line, I approached my healing from *all* angles, mind, body *and* spirit.

For the mind aspect, yes, I used meditation and visualization to clear my head space so that I could be present in the moment, in my body, and be vitally aware of my thoughts. I created a vision for my health, for my body, mind and spirit. And I can tell you that having a clear vision for every aspect of my life helped get me through some of my worst days of going through treatment.

I created a boundary with family and friends and communicated my "no negativity" policy. But I went far beyond maintaining a positive vibe. I also incorporated the "24 Hour Rule." When test results were coming in, I gave myself 24 hours to wrap my head around the results before discussing with *anyone*. This gave me space to absorb, feel and find solutions without the static of others' opinions.

I took *massive* action on my health vision. I educated myself and researched about my type of cancer, about my surgery, my treatment and side effects, about alternative and complementary treatments. I addressed the body and immediately changed my diet to 90 percent intake of alkaline foods and eliminated the acidic environment in my body. I exercised everyday whether I wanted to or not. I boosted my immune system through nutrition, supplements and acupuncture treatments. I found the best superfood nutrition, gentle detoxing methods and a medical device to improve my microcirculation while increasing my oxygen levels and removing metabolic waste from every cell in my body. This combination has allowed my body to thrive!

When I was going through cancer treatment I was constantly striving to make my spirit soar. I feel happiest when I am in nature, so I spent a lot of time at the beach with my toes in the sand, listening to the waves lap up on the shore and spotting the grace and magic of the dolphins.

And here's the good news! As of the writing of this book, I am six years cancer free. I am living my best life, shining beyond cancer!

For me, cancer was a profound, amazing, exhausting, emotional and enlightening journey. Today, I believe that whatever the condition of your physical body, right now you have the ability to overcome any symptom, condition or disease. But in my experience it will take more than a spiritual approach. It will require action and responsibility.

Hopefully, this chapter will inspire you to take a closer look at the vision you have for your foundation, your physical being, your body, your health. And then, once inspired, you will be prompted to take the necessary action to make that vision a reality.

Lisa Dimond is first and foremost the mother of two amazing, beautiful daughters. She has gone from mom to marketer to master trainer to Cancer Thriver Coach. Lisa is a serial entrepreneur and is currently the owner and master trainer of B-Vibrant Power Plate Studio, a powerful boutique fitness and wellness studio in Naples, FL. During Lisa's quest to return her body to optimal health following cancer treatment, she discovered a medical device called BEMER and today is an independent BEMER distributor, literally changing lives eight minutes at a time. Lisa's cancer journey and her innate desire to help others live their best life led her to partner with her dear friend and fellow cancer thriver, Marc Slugh, to co-author the book *Shine Beyond Cancer*. Together they founded a company under the same name, Shine Beyond Cancer, to take individuals from cancer survivor to cancer thriver using their VIP method which they share in their course Time To Shine. For more information: https://shinebeyondcancer.com/

Chapter 19

That we are souls on a journey is one of the most solid of spiritual beliefs. It is an unquestionable truth. And yet . . . is it true? For 50 years I held onto this belief. And then, in October 2007, an awakening blasted my world apart, and the existence of the soul was one of many precious "truths" that fell away in light of a higher, more unified understanding. I wanted to write about this because holding onto unquestioned truths (i.e. dogma) is an enormous block to spiritual evolution. Unfortunately, the very nature of dogma dictates that we rarely question it!

Cate Montana

The Soul And Other Assumptions

If you had asked me 13 years ago if I agreed with the ubiquitous (even innocuous) spiritual declaration, "You are a soul on a journey," I would have agreed. Forcefully even. Now? Well, it would depend upon the circumstances. If I were at a party or an after-services get-together in the reception hall at a Unity Church on a Sunday morning, I would most likely say something like, "Mmmm. Hey, did you try the meatballs? They're great."

I would be non-committal. I would change the subject. I wouldn't make waves. But as editor of this series of essays I can let it rip. Betsy and I didn't decide to publish a book about the stultifying effects of spiritual cliché-isms for nothing. So here goes.

Spirituality is nebulous

Spirituality, by its nature, is safely intangible. Anybody can pretty much say anything about anything and get away with it. "Wow. Did you notice that incredibly negative ball of energy that descended onto the planet last night around midnight from the 32nd dimension? It was gnarly!" Wow. Who am I to argue? Apparently I'm not sensitive enough to notice anything descending from the 32nd dimension. Maybe I need to meditate more and sharpen my faculties?

Yes, I jest, but only slightly. Anybody can say they experienced anything and nobody can gainsay their experience because 1) the nature of the "spiritual" realm is not the stuff that human beings, with our crippling dependency on the five physical senses to tell us what's what, can readily agree upon and 2) experience is subjective. Two people can stand side-by-side in a parking lot outside Costco. One sees the unmistakable face of Jesus in an approaching rain cloud and has an ecstatic experience while the person standing next to them sees a storm coming and worries about whether they closed the windows in the house before they left to go shopping.

The intangible, indefinable, ephemeral nature of the spirit world is why we've had religious wars and crusades and all sorts of theological disputes between people and nations for thousands of years. No one can decide whose god is the right god, or the most powerful god, or the most pervasive god or whether or not a particular god even exists. Nobody knows whether the prophet staggering out of the desert sandstorm raving about a burning bush is simply raving or actually saw something supernatural. We don't know whether an angel really appeared to Joseph or the Supreme Being appeared to Jacob and Isaac. There is rarely (if ever) corroborating testimony. Thus, we have two choices: either take the prophets' word that what they saw was divine or dismiss them altogether. Maybe they saw a UFO. Maybe the saw Marty McFly in the professor's DeLorean from *Back to the Future*. Maybe they saw God. Maybe they met a mentally advanced being with a less than humanitarian agenda. Maybe they're schizophrenic (as if we really know what that is either.)

We just don't, and cannot ever, know.

The most basic human need

The world's premiere inspirational coach and speaker, Tony Robbins, states there are six basic, universal needs that make human beings tick and drive all human behavior. And the first need, according to Robbins, is certainty.

To keep from going crazy in a topsy-turvy, unstable, ever-changing world, humans crave certainty and security above all else. In a reality where the only certainty is change, we desperately seek any port in the storm. This was especially so in ancient civilizations when there was no way to understand or reliably cope with environmental forces. Which is the fundamental reason religions, with their various and often conflicting "truths" and beliefs, have always been so popular. It doesn't matter how odd the premise: burning bushes, Paul's "third heaven," Ezekiel's vision of "wheels within wheels," claiming divine visitation always grabs people's attention. And whenever God shows up, a religion or belief system of some sort is never far behind, because stories give us a stable rock to cling to. They give us certainty where there is none. They give us a narrative to follow.

Transpersonal psychologist Dr. Abraham Maslow outlined a completely different hierarchy of human needs than Robbins, and one of the most basic needs in his system of thought is belonging. Humans are essentially communal creatures, like the monkeys and great apes we evolved from. In the wilds of nature, loners are vulnerable. Safety and survival are found in the herd. We naturally yearn to fit in, to have the security (there's that word again) that can only come when we belong to a group—whether it's a family, a church, a school, a village, a political party or a nation. And belonging to any group depends upon the certainty of shared stories and beliefs.

Which brings me to the New Age/New Thought community.

Like many, perhaps most, I prided myself when I left "the Church." I prided myself on having left stale religious dogma behind, vaulting into the rarified arena of the "real truth" at last. Enough with the unprovable stories about resurrection, mystical intervention, transubstantiation, sexual guilt, shame, and rigid rules. Little did I know 37 years ago when I walked into my first metaphysical book store that, although I was definitely broadening my spiritual horizons, I was about to trade one dogmatic realm for another.

My initial indoctrination came in 1981 when a highly psychic friend, a meteorologist at the TV station I worked at as a video production engineer in Atlanta, Georgia, offered to introduce me to my "guides." Certainly I was no stranger to the concept of guardian angels. But "guides"—eleven of which were apparently assigned to me because I was apparently something called a "light worker"—came as a surprise.

At first I was ecstatic about the whole thing. Someone I respected talked to angels and unseen spirits! And that someone said I was a special person, a spiritual person who had a spiritual mission here on Earth. And to help me with that mission I had eleven angelic helpers. Wow! I wasn't alone! There was more to the world than the eyes could see and the ears could hear. There was a higher purpose to my life and a higher truth to existence—if only I could avail myself of it.

And yet, after about a week, my logical left brain kicked in. Why in God's name would eleven angels bother sitting around up in heaven, cooling their jets, waiting for me to get my spiritual act together? And what would they do once I did and became aware of their presence? What would I do? Call on them to help me find a parking place? A better job? Another husband? More money? What a waste of resources!

It just didn't make sense. So, whether there were such things as guides or not, I let the concept go. But other things I never once thought to question.

The existence of the soul

The existence of the soul—some sort of ongoing, non-physical, aspect of "me" —the essence of self that confers individuality and eternal existence—has a long history. The Egyptians thought there were two aspects to the soul, the ba (the spirit body that entered the afterlife) and the ka (the breath which stayed near the body after death). The Greeks were divided on the subject, depending on which philosophical school you attended. The Hebrews believed the soul was part of the body. It wasn't until René Descartes came along in the 17th century and talked about the soul as a separate and distinct ongoing entity that the current Western spiritual concept of the soul as the "real" and spiritual aspect of the individual human came into popular acceptance.

Beliefs, once they become social institutions, are unconsciously taken as irrefutable, incontrovertible truths that only a crazy person or an ignoramus would dispute. And, once upon a time, such was the case with me when it came to the concept of the soul. As far as I was concerned, only an idiot didn't believe the soul existed. It did and that was that.

But then, an awakening experience in 2007 changed everything. (To be accurate, what occurred can't really be called an experience, because the word "experience" implies an *experiencer* "having" an experience, and the awakening experience itself made it very clear that there was no individual "I" to "have" anything, let alone an experience. Sigh. Such is the nature of divine truths. They cannot be communicated in normal language, if at all.)

Talk about a game changer!

Once it became clear that the "I"—the personal self that claimed the moniker Cate Montana—was truly an illusion, a figment of the mind that had no genuine substance or reality . . . once it became clear "I" was really life itself . . . pure awareness with no actual locale in time/space, the whole concept of the soul—that intangible eternal aspect of "me" that I had believed in unquestioningly my entire life—evaporated.

The jig was up. There was no "essence of me" that existed after death, because "me" was a complete illusion to start with.

When the mental perspective of "I" came back after three days of liberation, I was left trying to figure out why the hell "my" liberation wasn't permanent, why "I" came back, and how to live with my illusory self from that point forward. It was a hugely confusing time (even a despairing one) for about seven years. But even during the height of my confusion I never picked up the concept of the soul again.

Breaking free

The ego, the personal self we think we are, cannot imagine the personal self not existing. It's the single most terrifying concept going. Hence we make up stories. And the concept of the soul *as our ongoing spiritual essence*—the vehicle that will carry "me" forward from lifetime to lifetime—is very much a story. A good one. A comforting one. An edifying one. But a story none the less. For that which is spirit and immortal has no spiritual essence.

I wanted to talk about this for my chapter because if there is one constant in human existence, it's the universal desire for *more* . . . for expansion . . . for expression beyond limitations. It's why artists create. It's why entrepreneurs invent things. It's why spiritual seekers seek. And yet in the spiritual arena the nature of the mind makes expansion difficult. The illusion of the personal self, and yes, our beliefs in things like the existence of the soul, hold us back. We settle for beliefs not even knowing we're settling and then wonder why we feel like we're missing the ball somehow.

We feel like we're missing the ball because

we cling to stories about things we've never actually experienced.

I don't know about you, but although I believed in the soul wholeheartedly for over 50 years, I never once in my life *experienced* the soul. Have you? Oh, sure, I had tons of experiences sensing that there was something larger and completely ephemeral and eternal about me. Well, *duh*. Once the veil drops it's blindingly clear I am and always have been intangible spirit playing dress-up. Of course I sense I'm something more! But until I have the *experience* of my true nature I don't know it. And holding onto pretty beliefs is one of the things that keeps me from getting deep enough and raw enough and unencumbered enough to actually discover what I really am.

And it's not just a belief in the soul holding us back. My God, the spiritual community is rife with unprovable fluffy platitudes that millions of people end up wasting their entire lives holding onto—like the notions that "I am light." And "I am love." And "God is love."

Really? We know these things for a fact?

Okay, sure, quantum physics has proved there are no quantifiable boundaries between what appears to be you and what appears to be me. Everything in existence is pure energy. But there is more to this energetic sea of existence than "light" which is a very narrow bandwidth on the electromagnetic spectrum.

Maybe I see auras. Maybe I've been meditating and a brilliant, shining, ringing light shows up in my visual field and suddenly I'm overtaken with awe and ecstasy and a sense of overwhelming love. I am transported far far beyond my normal state of human consciousness. And when I come back I find myself on my knees believing I've been touched by God, or Jesus, or Allah, or Buddha, or the Archangel Michael. I take an expanded experience and immediately slap a label on it—I make up a story about it. And then I go around telling people what happened *as if I actually knew.*

Maybe I hear a commanding voice echoing out of the light that says, "I am the angel Moroni!" Yeah? How do I know that's who's behind the curtain? Do I take it at face value if some stranger walks up to me in a shopping mall and tells me that she's the reincarnation of Joan of Arc? What's the difference aside from the circumstances?

In truth, I don't know what happened at all. But the human mind is a meaning-making machine. And because humans need certainty, I make up meaning all the time. And then I live by the stories I make up. And die by them. And never go beyond them.

Love and compassion are normally the highest emotions a human being can experience. So we ascribe these things to heaven and to God and strive for them, never once realizing all we've done is shove God and heaven in a box and closed the lid. "God" or whatever you want to call the Source of All That Is, is apparently vastly beyond such things as "light" and "love." What a painful disservice to that which is unlimited to limit it to light and love! What a painful disservice to ourselves!

It is very much a truth that what we focus on we become. And light and love are charming things to focus upon. But to make them out to be more than they are and the penultimate expressions of the divine is, frankly, devastating. And to believe and hold fast to the notion that we are souls on a journey is to do nothing less than solidify the very construct we are trying to bust out of. For belief in the soul is predicated upon believing in our physical humanity. And to go on a journey is to validate and solidify the illusion of time and distance and separation.

I am spirit and nothing else. You are spirit and nothing else. Thinking otherwise is playing with illusion. There is no need for a soul when you already are forever. And going on a journey just perpetuates the painful notion that there is someplace else to go than right here, right now, being who and what you already are.

Cate Montana, MA is a dauntless explorer of inner and outer worlds. She has spent well over 20,000 hours meditating, has worked with plant medicines with shamans in the Amazon jungles of Peru, the Andes in Ecuador and the deserts of New Mexico, studied yoga in India, explored ancient South African ruins on horseback, hiked solo through England's sacred sites, shot raging rivers by kayak, camped alone across the US and Canada, lived for years alone in isolated cabins in the wilderness, raised wolves and trained Thoroughbred horses, married and divorced, and lots more. She is the author of the novel *Apollo & Me,* and several non-fiction works including, *The E Word: Ego, Enlightenment & Other Essentials* and *Unearthing Venus: My Search for the Woman Within* (Watkins). Author, inspirational speaker, journalist, editor, she lives on the island of Maui in the Hawaiian islands—the most isolated landmass in the world. For more information: www.catemontana.com